UNITED NATIONS CONFERENCE ON TRADE AND DEVELOPMENT
Geneva

D0775584

ECONOMIC DEVELOPMENT IN AFRICA

RECLAIMING POLICY SPACE

Domestic Resource Mobilization and Developmental States

UNITED NATIONS
New York and Geneva, 2007

NOTE

Symbols of United Nations documents are composed of capital letters combined with figures. Mention of such a symbol indicates a reference to a United Nations document.

The designations employed and the presentation of the material in this publication do not imply the expression of any opinion whatsoever on the part of the Secretariat of the United Nations concerning the legal status of any country, territory, city or area, or of its authorities, or concerning the delimitation of its frontiers or boundaries.

Material in this publication may be freely quoted or reprinted, but acknowledgement is requested, together with a reference to the document number. A copy of the publication containing the quotation or reprint should be sent to the UNCTAD secretariat.

UNCTAD/ALDC/AFRICA/2007

UNITED NATIONS PUBLICATION
Sales No. E.07.II.D.12
ISBN 978-92-1-112723-2
ISSN 1990–5114

ACKNOWLEDGEMENTS

This year's *Economic Development in Africa* report was prepared by a research team consisting of Samuel Gayi (team leader), Janvier Nkurunziza, Martin Halle and Shigehisa Kasahara. The first chapter drew upon the concept paper "Mobilizing non debt generating foreign and domestic resources for achieving the MDGs in Africa", prepared by Martin Brownbridge for an UNCTAD project on the same issue funded by the United Nations Development Account (fifth tranche). Detailed comments were received from Kamran Kousari and Martin Brownbridge on all the chapters, and from Chandra Patel on the policy conclusions. Diana Barrowclough reviewed the manuscript.

Statistical assistance was provided by a team from the Central Statistics and Information Retrieval Branch of the Division on Globalization and Development Strategies, UNCTAD, led by Flavine Creppy under the overall supervision of Henri Laurencin, Head, Central Statistics and Information Retrieval Branch.

The work was completed under the overall supervision of Habib Ouane, Director, Division for Africa, Least Developed Countries and Special Programmes in UNCTAD.

Heather Wicks provided secretarial support. Diego Oyarzun–Reyes designed the cover, and Michael Gibson edited the text. The overall layout, graphics and desktop publishing were done by Madasamyraja Rajalingam.

CONTENTS

Explanatory notes vi
Abbreviations vi

INTRODUCTION 1

CHAPTER 1
DOMESTIC RESOURCE MOBILIZATION: ISSUES AT STAKE 6

  A.   Domestic resources 6
  B.   Trends in savings.. 7
  C.   Household savings... 10
  D.   Corporate savings 14
  E.   Public sector revenue: taxation 16
  F.   Financial markets and intermediation 19
  G.   Workers' remittances... 25
  H.   Capital flight.. 29
  I.   Conclusion 31

CHAPTER 2
THE CHALLENGE OF INCREASING SAVINGS AND BOOSTING PRODUCTIVE INVESTMENT 33

  A.   Introduction 33
  B.   Increasing savings 34
  C.   Credit constraints... 41
  D.   Barriers to investment in Africa 46
  E.   Effect of business environment on gross domestic capital formation 53

CHAPTER 3
TOWARDS A "DEVELOPMENTAL STATE" 57

  A.   Introduction 57
  B.   The developmental State: concept and characteristics 58
  C.   Financial sector reforms: curbing government intervention
        to cure "financial repression" 65
  D.   Can Africa nurture "developmental States"?................................. 74

E. "Policy space" – what to do with it? 84
F. Concluding remarks 87

CHAPTER 4
RECLAIMING AND UTILIZING POLICY SPACE **89**

A. Mobilizing domestic savings 90
B. Developing credit markets and boosting productive investments 93
C. Delivering appropriate financial and investment policies:
    the need for a "developmental State" 95

NOTES **99**
REFERENCES **106**

LIST OF BOXES

1. Newly industrializing economies: dynamics of capital accumulation,
   export–investment nexus and rent management 62
2. The role of central banks in development 68

LIST OF FIGURES

1. Gross domestic savings in sub-Saharan Africa, 1960–2005 8
2. Gross domestic savings by developing regions, 1960–2004 9
3. Selected indicators of financial depth and financial intermediation 20
4. Capital flows to Africa, 1985–2005 27
5. Capital formation vs. business environment 54

LIST OF TABLES

1. Distribution of savings rates in Africa, 2000–2005 8
2. Regional comparative data on the cost of doing business 46
3. Gross national savings, gross domestic investment and exports
   in the Asian NIEs and Africa, 1971–2005 64
4. Mind the technology gap: East Asia and Africa 66
5. Per capita GDP growth rates: top 50 developing countries, 1960–1975 79
6. Economic performance by period and region 81

EXPLANATORY NOTES

The $ sign refers to the United States dollar.

Sub-Saharan Africa (SSA): Except where otherwise stated, this includes South Africa.

North Africa: Unlike in the UNCTAD *Handbook of Statistics*, in this publication Sudan is classified as part of sub-Saharan Africa, not North Africa.

ABBREVIATIONS

APRM	African Peer Review Mechanism
FDI	foreign direct investment
GATT	General Agreement on Tariffs and Trade
GDP	gross domestic product
GERD	gross expenditure on research and development
GNI	gross national income
ICT	information and communication technology
IMF	International Monetary Fund
ISI	import substituting industrialization
MDGs	Millennium Development Goals
NEPAD	New Partnership for Africa's Development
NIEs	newly industrializing economies
ODA	official development assistance
OECD	Organization for Economic Cooperation and Development
REI	rigidity of employment index
SAP	structural adjustment programme
WTO	World Trade Organization

INTRODUCTION

One of the most prominent objectives of the Millennium Development Goals (MDGs) adopted at the United Nations Millennium Summit in 2000 was to have member States halve their levels of absolute poverty by 2015. While some regions of the developing world have made sufficient progress towards achieving this goal, sub-Saharan Africa has been singled out as one region that is unlikely to meet the target by 2015 if current trends continue. Indeed, halfway through to the target year, the latest data on poverty shows that sub-Saharan Africa is the only developing region where the absolute number of poor people has been steadily increasing, even if the relative number declined from 47 per cent to 41 per cent of the total population between 1999 and 2004 (Chen and Ravaillon, 2007). One of the reasons why sub-Saharan Africa might miss the 2015 target is its relatively low rate of economic growth. Indeed, despite the recent gains made by a number of countries in terms of export revenue, thanks to high prices of some major primary commodities, the growth rate in sub-Saharan Africa as a region continues to fall short of the 7–8 per cent necessary to achieve the MDGs target on halving poverty.

To raise the growth rate and sustain it at the level that will allow African countries to halve poverty by 2015 requires a significant increase in the volume of foreign and domestic resources devoted to promoting overall development in general, and poverty reduction programmes in particular. There have been numerous international initiatives aimed at increasing the volume of official development assistance (ODA) and its grant element to poor countries.[1] However, donors are not on course to meet these pledges (OXFAM, 2007; The Economist, 2007), and the overall effect of these resources on poverty reduction has remained marginal. The limited development effectiveness of ODA has been partly associated with the inefficiency in the use of aid, which has resulted in relatively small amounts effectively used for development purposes (UNCTAD, 2006a). Foreign direct investment (FDI) flows to Africa, though on the increase in recent years, are still too limited in geographical coverage and focused on extractive industries to have a significant effect on employment creation and poverty alleviation (UNCTAD, 2005). In this regard, harnessing domestic financial resources could help raise additional financing in order to narrow Africa's resource gap and accelerate the process of economic development and poverty reduction. Moreover, reducing dependence on donor funds and associated conditionalities would increase "ownership" of the development process whereby these resources could be used to fund countries' own priorities rather than those of the donors.

There are several potential sources of domestic finance that could provide important additional development resources if they were properly tapped. However, the policy actions taken so far to increase the total development resource envelope do not sufficiently recognize that African countries need to step up their efforts at enhancing domestic resource mobilization. Firstly, some public finance reforms have been implemented to increase government revenue, but they have been limited to basic issues such as the introduction of broad-based consumption taxes, mainly in the form of value added tax. The effect on government revenue has remained limited. Secondly, little effort has been made to mobilize workers' remittances, a major external resource for a number of African countries. Currently, the flows of remittances largely bypass the banking system. They are channeled into consumption and, to some extent, real estate development, with little positive impact on development. Thirdly, there have been no concerted efforts to tap investible resources from the large and vibrant informal sector in African countries. Fourthly, capital flight continues to deny African economies large amounts of the continent's own resources that could have funded domestic investments that create jobs and provide or boost incomes of the large segments of the population that are unemployed or underemployed. Fifthly, the reforms in the financial sector have focused on interest rate liberalization and the dismantling of entry barriers in the banking sector to increase competition in order to improve the quality of financial intermediation. So far, the results have been mixed.

Africa's financial resources needs

African economies have been enjoying a period of relatively strong economic performance over the past few years. This is an encouraging change from the previous decades, when economic performance was either negative or stagnating. The growth rate for the continent was 5.7 per cent in 2006, exceeding even the record rates of 5.3 per cent in 2005 and 5.2 per cent in 2004 (UNECA, 2007). The sub-Saharan African region, meanwhile, recorded a per capita gross domestic product (GDP) growth rate of 3.4 per cent in 2005, the highest since 1974 (World Bank, 2007a). This impressive performance is principally due to rising prices for primary commodities, benefits from macroeconomic stability and reform, substantial inflows of external financing and debt relief (UNECA, 2007).

Despite strong macroeconomic performance since the turn of the century, the growth rates achieved are still insufficient for the continent to achieve the objectives of the MDGs by the target date of 2015. From 1998 to 2006, only five countries in Africa (Angola, Chad, Equatorial Guinea, Mozambique and Sudan) grew at 7–8 per cent growth rates necessary for halving poverty (UNECA, 2007). Additionally, although the region as a whole has enjoyed good economic performance in recent years, growth rates remain dependent on a small number of primary commodities and high average growth rates mask large differences in performance across the region. Furthermore, recent economic growth has not translated into corresponding increases in employment, and the limited job creation that has taken place has mainly been in the informal sector, due to the capital-intensive and enclave nature of the extractive sectors that have been driving this growth (UNCTAD, 2005; ILO, 2007). This phenomenon of "jobless growth" is a major preoccupation of African Ministers of Finance, Planning and Economic Development, as expressed in Abuja in 2005 (UNECA, 2005b).

Policy choices, political stability and the external environment all play crucial roles in defining the economic performance of African countries. Regardless of the situation, however, the availability of resources for socially and economically productive investment will be a necessary condition for a more balanced growth trajectory based on economic diversification (UNCTAD, 2003) and employment creation. Current resources are neither sufficient nor stable enough to allow the region to fully attain the first Millennium Development Goal by 2015 (UNCTAD, 2000a; UNCTAD, 2005; UNCTAD, 2006a; UNECA, 2006).

Estimating the cost in resources of achieving the MDGs is necessarily a speculative exercise. These estimates do, however, point to the order of magnitude of the existing resource gap. It is believed that, across all developing countries, an additional $50 billion to $76 billion per year is needed to reach the MDGs. In Africa, the need for additional resources is generally believed to amount to between 10 and 20 per cent of GDP (UNECA, 2005a; UNECA, 2006; see UNCTAD, 2006a for more information on cost estimates).

UNCTAD estimated in 2000 that investment rates needed to reach 22–25 per cent in order to increase sustainable growth rates to 6 per cent (UNCTAD, 2000a). From 2000 to 2004, sub-Saharan Africa averaged investment rates of only 18.1 per cent of GDP, while the figure for all of Africa was 20.7 per cent. Explanations for these low rates tend to highlight the low savings rates as well as the lack of profitable investment opportunities. Only seven countries in sub-Saharan Africa (Botswana, Chad, Eritrea, Gabon, Lesotho, Mozambique, and Sao Tome and Principe) achieved investment rates above 25 per cent of GDP. In North Africa, however, investment rates were notably higher, averaging 25.6 per cent (World Bank, 2006).

The resource gap in Africa must be bridged using both external and domestic resources. There are, however, a number of problems related to excessive dependence on foreign capital flows (see UNCTAD, 2005; UNCTAD, 2006a). Strengthening of domestic resource mobilization, combined with improvements in the efficiency and efficacy in the use of such resources, will not only reduce or eliminate the resource gap. It will also increase the "policy space" available to the State to enable it to define its development goals and the means to attain them.

The objective of this year's report is to examine the potential of African countries to increase their total domestic resource envelope in order to reduce dependence on external resources, namely ODA, and diversify their development resources. Channelling these resources to productive investments to increase their efficiency is a complementary objective. To achieve these aims, the State will have to assume its role as a "developmental State", a concept that this report intends to bring back to centre stage (see chapter 3 for a discussion of this concept). Indeed, the African State must reclaim its developmental role in order to give true meaning to the rhetoric of "ownership" in macroeconomic and resource management.

Of course, resource mobilization will not by itself solve all the problems faced by African countries, particularly considering that many of them lack the institutions and human resources necessary to make development work. However, in the medium to long term, the ability of African countries to finance an increasing share of their development needs from domestic sources would give them much-needed flexibility in the formulation and implementation of policies that address their economic, social and other developmental challenges. The multiplicity of the challenges facing Africa inevitably calls for an appropriate "policy mix" or "diversity of policies" tailored to the specific situation of each country, rather than a one-size-fits-all approach. In this context, the report highlights the need for more policy space for African countries to design and implement policies that make optimal use of available resources in a way that leads to a virtuous circle of accumulation, investment, growth and poverty reduction drawing on the model of developmental States.

Chapter 1 is a brief exposé of the salient issues involved in domestic resource mobilization within the context of African countries. Chapter 2 examines the challenges involved in raising the level of savings in Africa and discusses how the savings raised could be used to finance productive investments as a basis for sustainable growth. Chapter 3 delineates the characteristics of "developmental States" while examining their applicability to Africa. It argues that the necessary conditions are currently in place for African countries to tackle their developmental challenges within the framework of a "developmental State". Chapter 4, the final chapter, distils some policy conclusions from the preceding discussions.

Chapter 1

DOMESTIC RESOURCE MOBILIZATION: ISSUES AT STAKE

A. Domestic resources

Low levels of domestic resource mobilization are believed to be caused by low levels of income, demographic factors and the structure of financial markets, which are generally difficult to influence in the short to medium term. It has often been assumed, therefore, that it is unrealistic to expect a large and sustained increase in domestic resource mobilization in Africa. As a result, increasing domestic resource mobilization has been described as the "hard option" for closing Africa's resource gap (Aryeetey, 2004). Discussions on how to fill the resource gap have consequently tended to focus heavily on the increase of external flows such as ODA and FDI, as well as on debt reduction.

Such a focus is problematic in the African context for several reasons. ODA, while it remains a major source of finance in the region, is volatile, heavily concentrated and dependent on the priorities (often geopolitical or strategic, including security considerations) of development partners (UNCTAD, 2006a). FDI, which has attracted a lot of attention recently, is even more highly concentrated in Africa than is ODA. FDI is also relatively volatile and tends to focus on extractive industries with very few linkages to the domestic economy (UNCTAD, 2005). Portfolio investment, with the exception of South Africa, is of insignificant magnitude in the region (UNECA, 2006).

Strengthening domestic resource mobilization offers many potential benefits to African economies. Firstly, it will reduce the dependency on external flows, thereby reducing one of the sources of damaging volatility in resource availability, and reduce vulnerability to external shocks. Secondly, it will give African countries greater policy space, increasing their ownership of the development process as well as strengthening their State capacity. Thirdly, successful endeavours to increase the importance of domestic resources in the development process depend on the State's ability to improve the domestic economic environment, creating important positive externalities. Finally, these efforts are also likely to be seen as a positive sign by donors and investors, thereby augmenting external resource inflows.

Three distinct issues must be considered for domestic resources to play an increased role in the economic development of African countries. Firstly, there is the matter of the amount of existing resources. Secondly, these resources must be held in a form that facilitates economically and socially beneficial allocation. Finally, available resources must be used effectively and efficiently.

The principal sources of domestic resources are private savings and government revenue. Workers' remittances, though not generated domestically, can represent a significant source of domestic resources once in the receiving country. Conversely, capital flight directly reduces the amount of domestic resources available for investment. It is important to examine these financial flows in our analysis of the total volume of domestic resource availability, as their impact could be positive, as in the case of remittances, or negative, as in the case of capital flight.

B. Trends in savings

Sub-Saharan Africa has the lowest savings rate of any developing region. In 2005, gross domestic savings in the region represented 17.6 per cent of GDP, compared with 26.0 per cent in South Asia, 24.0 per cent in Latin America and the Caribbean, and nearly 42.9 per cent in East Asia and Pacific countries (World Bank, 2007a).

This average savings rate for Africa, however, masks important disparities across the continent. In 2005, Algeria and the Republic of the Congo both achieved gross domestic savings rates of more than 50 per cent of their GDP, while Eritrea and Sao Tome and Principe both had rates far below minus 20 per cent, indicating dissaving on a massive scale (World Bank, 2006).

The savings rate for sub-Saharan Africa has broadly evolved over the years in the following pattern. From 1960 to 1974, it increased steadily from 17.5 per cent to 24.3 per cent of GDP (World Bank, 2007a). It then experienced much higher volatility before reaching its highest rate (nearly 26 per cent) in 1980. Then came Africa's "savings collapse" (Eldabawi and Mwega, 2000), as the rate fell to under 15 per cent in 1992. Since then, there has been a tentative recovery, yet the rate has remained low, and was only 17.6 per cent in 2005 (World Bank, 2007a).

Table 1
Distribution of savings rates in Africa, 2000–2005
(Number of countries)

Negative	0–10% of GDP	10–20% of GDP	20–30% of GDP	Over 30% of GDP
11	14	13	7	5

Source: World Development Indicators, 2007.

Figure 1
Gross domestic savings in sub-Saharan Africa, 1960–2005
(Percentage of GDP)

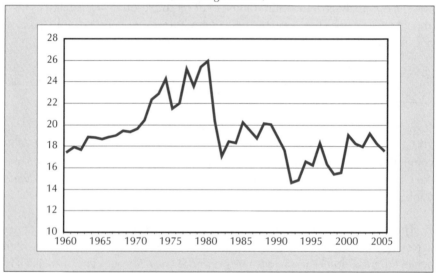

Source: World Development Indicators, 2007.

The trend has also been one of increasing disparity between developing regions, especially after 1980. Africa's saving rates have fallen, Latin America's have stagnated and East Asia's rates soared. These trends mirror the general economic performance of these regions over the past four decades or so (Hussein and Thirlwall, 1999).

In addition to savings rates, stability over time is crucial for smooth and predictable investment, and Africa again fares worse than other developing regions in this area. A major reason for this is the volatility of the sources of income, which is higher in Africa than in other developing regions, due mainly to exogenous shocks. The standard deviation for gross national savings as a share of GDP from 1965 to 1992 was 8.7 per cent for Africa, 6.6 per cent for the East Asian "Tigers" and 6.0 per cent for Latin America and the Caribbean (Schmidt-Hebbel et al., 1994).

The *capacity* to save is mainly determined by income level, rate of income growth and the dependency ratio, i.e. the ratio of population under 16 or above 60 years old to that of the working-age population (Loayza et al., 2000). A positive relationship exists between savings rate and per capita income (Hussein and Thirlwall, 1999). Savings rates have also been found to increase in response to rises in the rate of growth of per capita income. Finally, savings rates appear to respond negatively to increases in the dependency ratio.

Willingness to save, meanwhile, is believed to depend on the ease of access to savings instruments, the attractiveness of such instruments and the prevailing economic conditions (Wright, 1999; Hussein and Thirlwall, 1999).

Figure 2

Gross domestic savings by developing regions, 1960–2004

(Percentage of GDP)

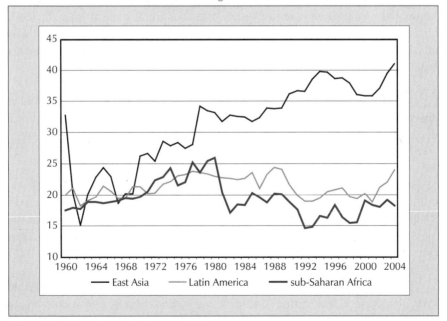

Source: World Development Indicators, 2007.

Gross savings rates provide a useful insight into the general picture of savings in a national economy. They are not, however, necessarily reliable indicators of the domestic resources available for investment in African countries. This is partly due to problems of accuracy in the national account data for savings. Indeed, the calculation method, which derives savings as a residual from other variables, yields high margins of error (Deaton, 1990). In addition, private saving in African countries is often precautionary in nature and is inadequately captured by national account data (Aryeetey and Udry, 2000).

Considering that savings can exist in many different forms, the nature of savings instruments has a large impact on the possibilities for transforming savings into productive investments. To understand the nature of savings and their relation to investment, it is necessary to look into the details of saving options and choices at the household and firm levels.

C. Household savings

Improving the mobilization of household savings could free up significant amounts of resources for investments that promote development. Indeed, household savings dominate savings in Africa but are at present not sufficiently channelled into productive use (Aryeetey and Udry, 2000). Understanding why and how households save, especially poorer households, can help to identify policies that increase the amount of resources available for development.

Households, especially in rural areas, rely on volatile income sources. In the absence of accessible credit and insurance services, drawing on saved assets is a necessary strategy for households to smooth their consumption patterns (Deaton, 1990; Dercon, 2002).

Saving as a precaution implies that even at low disposable income levels and in the absence of attractive savings instruments, poor households need to save a substantial part of their income. In Ghana, for example, it was found that the median household in rural areas in the South of the country saved over 30 per cent of their income (Aryeetey and Udry, 2000).

This kind of precautionary saving is the main motivation for household saving in Africa. Research from Ghana shows that financial savings increase with income only in the wealthiest 10 per cent of households (Aryeetey, 2004). This suggests that for a large proportion of households, saving is a necessary form of self-insurance. This has important implications both for the pattern of saving that it generates and for the asset choice of households. The pattern of household saving tends to be irregular, with frequent swings between saving and dissaving. This irregular saving pattern tends to generate a preference for saving instruments that are highly liquid and accessible (Deaton, 1990).

Saving instruments for households fall into four categories: non-financial savings, informal financial savings, formal financial savings and semi-formal financial savings. The composition of household savings portfolio determines availability of funds for investment, and is therefore relevant to a country's development.

In Africa, household savings consist mainly of physical assets and some financial savings held in the informal financial sector. Thus, only a small part is available for productive investment.

Non-financial savings

Households often hold considerable diverse portfolios of non-financial assets, such as livestock, stocks of goods for trading, grain and construction materials that are acquired as stores of wealth, and are often bought or sold in such a way as to smooth consumption patterns. While the evidence is limited, studies suggest that non-financial assets represent around 80 per cent of all household assets in rural areas (Aryeetey and Udry, 2000).

The choice of non-financial assets as saving instruments can reflect a variety of factors. Some non-financial assets, such as livestock, real estate or jewelry, carry symbolic value or serve as indicators of status and/or wealth. The accumulation of non-financial assets as saving instruments, however, can also reflect rational portfolio decision in a context of high risk, uncertain financial environment and lack of access to adequate financial instruments. Thus, whilst a certain amount of non-financial assets is likely to remain as a part of the saving portfolio of households in African countries, an improvement in access, adequacy and reliability on the part of the financial sector could trigger an increase in savings held in a financial form through substitution from non-financial to financial saving instruments.

Informal financial savings

The informal financial sector offers a wide range of saving instruments, from simple deposit collection to large, self-organized saving groups and saving pools (Wright, 1999). Mostly, savings tend to be made in small but frequent deposits that correspond to the needs of households and small businesses. Problems of access and reliability are limited in comparison to the formal financial sector as informal financial institutions operate in geographically and socially confined community settings (Nissanke and Aryeetey, 2006).

In contrast to the formal financial sector, it is rare for informal sector savings to accrue interest. Resources mobilized through saving in the informal sector are generally not used for further investment and therefore tend not to generate any income. In most cases therefore, depositors are required pay for the saving service. The fact that poorer households save despite receiving what are in effect negative interests is testimony to the importance of saving services for poorer households and to the willingness of such households to save. Households in Africa tend to combine a number of saving instruments with different institutions, offering different deposit and withdrawal conditions. This helps them spread default risk and meet their changing need for financial resources (Wright, 1999).

Formal financial savings

In sub-Saharan Africa, savings held in the formal financial sector generally represent a small proportion of household assets. Evidence from Northern Ghana suggests that, of the 20 per cent of household assets that are held in financial form, 12 per cent are held in the informal sector and 8 per cent in the formal sector (Aryeetey, 2004). This reflects the difficulties in access to formal saving instruments and, more importantly, the lack of trust in formal financial institutions, as well as the inadequacy of formal saving instruments to fulfil poorer households' savings needs.

Banks are the principal type of formal financial institutions engaging in savings mobilization in Africa. In some countries, post office branches have also been used, taking advantage of their extended network. Recent reforms to the financial sector in many African countries have led to a reduction in branch numbers as banks, free from government interference, have focused on more profitable often urban-based activities even though an increase in branches in rural areas could promote savings in the formal financial sector (Ikhide, 1996).

Physical distance from banking institutions is not the only limiting factor to the growth of formal financial savings. High minimum deposit and balance requirements, the time that it takes to make transactions and the administrative work involved also discourage depositors. Furthermore, the reluctance of banks to provide credit to poorer households and small businesses lessens the incentive to save in the formal sector (Wright, 1999).

There are some encouraging signs, however, that technology may be able to overcome some of the remoteness and processing-cost barriers to providing services to poor and rural areas. Mobile phone banking enables banks to provide basic financial services to poor people, including in rural areas. Though it is only a recent development, mobile phone banking is already reaching thousands of customers in countries such as Botswana, Kenya and Zambia (Honohan and Beck, 2007). [2]

The level of trust in banking institutions is low in most African countries. Banks have been subject to pervasive government intervention in their operations, especially before the recent financial sector reforms. Political expediency was often preferred to commercial viability, resulting in banks having enormous liabilities threatening their operations. Banking crises beset many African countries between the mid-1980s and mid-1990s. In their review of banking crises in 10 African countries between 1985 and 1995, Daumont et al. (2004) found that non-performing loans exceeded 50 per cent of total loans in Benin, Cameroon, Côte d'Ivoire, Guinea, Senegal, Uganda and the United Republic of Tanzania, with Ghana and Nigeria not far behind. In many countries, these crises were large enough to deeply affect the national economy. In Benin, for example, the banking crisis of 1988–1990 saw all three of the country's banks collapse due to 78 per cent of their loans being non-performing, resulting in an estimated cost to the economy of 17 per cent of GDP. The most important features behind banking crises in Africa have been extensive government interference, poor banking supervision and regulation, and shortcomings in management (Daumont et al., 2004).

Despite reforms, banks have not noticeably improved their loan portfolios, and public trust has not improved. The saving that does take place in the formal sector generally favours short-term deposit accounts and the proportion of savings held in longer-term deposit instruments remains low (Nissanke and Aryeetey, 1998).

Semi-formal financial savings

An emerging semi-formal financial sector in Africa specializes in providing financial services to households and small businesses that do not have access to formal financial institutions. This sector is made up of institutions that, while legally registered, are not regulated as banks. While this semi-formal sector could become an important actor in savings mobilization for households, its coverage is at present too limited to respond effectively to the financial needs of many households in Africa.

The semi-formal sector, however, holds great potential in terms of improved savings mobilization in the region. Indeed, if semi-formal institutions succeed in offering safe and reasonably liquid savings instruments that generate positive returns for many households, there could be a substantial increase in financial savings available for profitable investments due to reallocation from both non-financial assets and financial assets currently held in the informal sector.

In sum, the choice of saving instrument reflects issues of access, reliability and relevance of available saving instruments to meeting households' saving needs. Households in Africa save essentially for precautionary reasons. The assets they hold are substitutes for insurance and credit, which are not available to them. The saving pattern thus created is one of irregular and short-term saving in which, over time, there can be as much saving as dissaving (Deaton, 1990). The financial requirements of households therefore call for safe saving instruments that allow small transactions at frequent intervals. The very high proportion of non-financial assets in household savings portfolios suggests that the financial sector is currently not adequately fulfilling these needs.

D. Corporate savings

Corporate savings have received much less attention than household savings and remain an area that is generally underresearched, particularly with regard to developing countries. In most African countries, the data necessary to disaggregate private savings into household and corporate components is unavailable. One of the few countries in Africa with sufficient data to permit a detailed examination of corporate savings is South Africa. Evidence in this case suggests that corporate savings respond to changes in the rate of profits, inflation, interest rates and availability of credit (Aron and Muellbauer, 2000). The corporate and financial sectors in South Africa are, however, markedly more developed than those in most

African countries. There are therefore serious limitations to the transferability of these findings to other countries in the region.

In most African countries, the corporate sector is strongly dualistic, with a small number of legally registered firms and a much larger number of enterprises operating in the informal sector. The limited information that exists on the corporate sector in the region too often focuses only on the first category, giving a distorted view of the reality facing most enterprises.

Large firms are much more likely than small or micro firms to receive bank loans (Bigsten et al., 2003). Access and cost of financing are problems for most enterprises in Africa, however. This is especially the case for the small domestic enterprises in the informal sector that represent the vast majority of firms in the region[3]. As a result, firms are dependent on their retained earnings to fund not only their working capital but also new investments. Firms in sub-Saharan Africa fund between one half and three quarters of their new investments from their internal savings (Nasir et al., 2003; Blattman et al., 2004; World Bank, 2007b).

Corporate savings are therefore essential to the security and growth of firms. Faced with a financial system that does not meet their needs, firms have to depend on their own savings to insure against temporary falls in earnings and to fund further development. Fafchamps et al. (2000) found that, in Zimbabwe, firms use large inventory stocks and, to a lesser extent, financial savings as self-insurance in the face of a risky operational environment. Given the crucial role of savings for the firms that produce them, there can be very little intermediation of these funds towards other purposes. Indeed, the inability of many firms to secure outside financing means that savings will need to be either directly reinvested in the firm that produces them, or kept in highly liquid form in order to be easily accessible in times of need.

Financing new investments from retained earnings can be highly efficient. In fact, as savings are made up of retained profits, they are often primarily generated by successful and profitable enterprises that are therefore reasonably unlikely to invest in low-yielding investments.

There are nonetheless reasons to believe that the current situation of corporate savings and investment in Africa is far from optimal. Firstly, the number of firms that are credit-constrained testifies to the fact that their retained earnings are not a sufficient source of funds to meet their perceived needs (Bigsten et al., 2003). This is borne out by the fact that the graduation rate from micro to more complex enterprises is lower in Africa than in other regions (Nissanke, 2001). Secondly, self-investment may be productive, but other investment opportunities might be more profitable or more suited to the firms' immediate needs. Finally, the lack of credit and insurance possibilities for many firms means that savings need to be kept in highly liquid form and can therefore not be easily reinvested by the financial system into productive investment. The current situation therefore not only constrains the growth of firms, but also contributes to low levels of development of the financial sector.

A financial system that better meets firms' financial needs may lower the level of savings that occur for self-insurance and self-investment reasons. On the other hand, it is likely to make available a much larger proportion of corporate savings for productive investment.

E. Public sector revenue: taxation

The amount and efficiency of government spending is an essential part of making domestic resources the engine of African development. Public sector resources have a distinct and complementary role to play vis-à-vis private savings. While a distinction can be made between public expenditure, which covers recurrent costs, and public savings, which fund longer-term investments, the needs that both address are immense in most African countries. Public expenditure is essential to human capital development through its funding of essential public services such as education and health care. Public investment, on the other hand, can provide the resources for infrastructure that is indispensable for the private sector to thrive.

The balance between expenditure and investment therefore matters less than the amount of resources involved and the efficiency with which they are utilized. Taxes account for almost all of government revenue in most African countries. Increasing tax revenue can therefore have a significant impact on improving domestic resource mobilization provided it does so without discouraging private economic activity.

The amount of tax revenue as a percentage of GDP in Africa was 22 per cent in 2002 (World Bank, 2005a). This is lower than the average for developed countries. Europe/ Organization for Economic Cooperation and Development (OECD) had rates of 32 per cent for the same year. Africa's tax ratio, however, is higher than that of other developing regions (Tanzi and Zee, 2000), although there are considerable differences within the region. The tax ratio is considerably lower in sub-Saharan Africa (20 per cent) than in North Africa (25 per cent). Moreover, if South Africa is excluded, the tax ratio for sub-Saharan Africa is only 16 per cent (World Bank, 2005a). Furthermore, there are important differences between countries in the region with regard to their tax performance. Tax as a share of GDP in 2002 ranged from more than 38 per cent in Algeria and Angola to less than 10 per cent in Chad, Niger and Sudan (World Bank, 2005a).

The tax-to-GDP ratio in a given economy is broadly determined by a set of structural features. Chief among these are the level of per capita income, urbanization, literacy, the shares of the industrial, agricultural and mining sectors, as well as the importance of trade (Tanzi and Zee, 2000).

In sub-Saharan Africa specifically, the main determinants of the tax-to-GDP ratio have been found to be per capita income, trade levels, and the shares of agriculture and mining in the economy (Stotsky and WoldeMariam, 1997). Per capita income reflects not only the taxable capacity of the population, it also serves as an indicator for the general development of an economy. For both these reasons, per capita GDP has been found to be positively correlated to higher tax to GDP ratios. Although they have been decreasing in recent years due to trade liberalization, taxes on trade remain important sources of revenue for African States. Levels of exports and imports are therefore both positively correlated with higher taxes. The share of agriculture in the economy has been found to have a significant and negative effect on the tax-to-GDP ratio. Agriculture in African countries is mainly carried out by small farmers who operate in the informal sector and generate only small levels of taxable income. The share of mining in the economy has also been found to have a negative effect on taxes, although the reasons for this are unclear (Stotsky and WoldeMariam, 1997).

One way of comparing taxation across different countries is to determine the tax share that can be "expected" in a country given the various determinants. This expected tax-to-GDP ratio is then compared to the actual one. This is known as the "tax effort". The international comparison of tax efforts carried out by Piancastelli (2001) finds that the tax effort is higher in Africa than in other regions, despite the low tax-to-GDP ratios achieved. This would suggest that the tax rates achieved in Africa, while low, are higher than expected given the structure and development levels of African economies. However, measures of tax effort are strongly dependent on the model used to determine the expected tax rate, so tax effort measures suffer from serious limitations and are at best indicative.

High tax-to-GDP ratios are not necessarily a measure of a successful tax system. Rather, fiscal policy is about who gets what from the State, how public spending is financed and who pays for it (Addison et al., 2006). As such, it is at the heart of the wider problem of resource mobilization and use. Public revenue should be mobilized in a way that preserves incentives for private sector actors to work and save. An optimal tax system should strive for equity, efficiency and administrative convenience (Thirlwall, 2003).

The tax reforms that many African countries have undertaken in the past two decades have tended to treat taxation as a technical and administrative exercise, ignoring its political nature. These reforms have mainly been donor-driven and have sought to change the composition of taxation to favour taxes that are easier to collect and perceived to be less distorting to the economy. Typically, this has translated into a focus on indirect taxes such as value added tax, a reduction of direct tax rates combined with measures to increase their reach, and a reduction of the importance of taxes on international trade. On the administrative side, reforms have concentrated on trying to enhance the institutional capacity of tax administration by increasing the number and salary of staff, training, technical equipment and simplification of procedures.

These reforms, however, have had limited success in increasing the tax revenue of African countries. It is, of course, essential to improve the technical and administrative aspects of taxation, especially improving the capacity of tax administrations and tackling corruption. By focusing exclusively on those aspects, however, the reforms have ignored the fact that taxation represents a political relation between the State and society (DiJohn, 2006).

The low tax levels in Africa are in part due to features that make tax collection more difficult. These include low levels of per capita income; large agricultural sectors; and a sizeable share of production, transactions and employment taking place in the informal economy, which in 2001 was estimated to account for 78 per cent of non-agricultural employment in Africa (Xaba et al., 2002). Low tax rates also represent a relative weakness of the State with regard to certain sections of the society. Taxable capacity in Africa tends to be highly concentrated in a small number of people and firms that can often evade taxes by using their power and influence. The majority of the population, while it may not have much political power and influence, typically has low taxable capacity that is costly to collect, especially in rural areas (Fjeldstad and Rakner, 2003; Fjeldstad, 2006). In Uganda, for example, only middle-size firms tend to pay taxes. Large firms can use their influence and relations within the State to evade taxes and small firms can dodge taxes by staying in the informal sector (Gauthier and Reinikka, 2006).

State legitimacy is ultimately at the heart of taxation. Applying criteria of efficiency, effectiveness and fairness not only to the tax system but also to the use of government resources can create a virtuous cycle of improving fiscal performance, service delivery and state legitimacy. Recent research in the United Republic of Tanzania, for example, reveals that a large majority is willing to pay more taxes if the resources visibly improve public services (Fjeldstad, 2006). Thus, while reforming the tax system is an essential part of improving domestic resource mobilization, it is unlikely to succeed in the absence of more profound changes to State–society relations.

F. Financial markets and intermediation

Financial intermediation provides the crucial link between savings and investment. A well-functioning financial system should be able to mobilize resources effectively and allocate them to the most productive investment opportunities. Without effective financial intermediation, the incentive to hold financial savings is depressed and investment tends to concentrate on the sector in which the savings take place, which may not be the most productive. As a result, there are fewer resources mobilized and these are allocated to less productive investments.

The demand for financial services in Africa is high, despite the low income levels. Households need financial services to manage the risks linked to the volatility of their income sources, and firms need financing in order to grow. The financial system in Africa, however, has largely failed to meet the demand for efficient financial intermediation.

Central to the failure to meet these needs is the fragmented and segmented structure of the financial sector in Africa. Financial services tend to be provided mainly by a small formal financial sector that concentrates on the higher market-end, and a larger informal financial sector that concentrates on the lower market-end. There is very little interaction between the two sectors and there is a considerable gap in the financial services market in between the two market-ends.

The formal financial sector

The formal financial sector in Africa, as in other regions of the developing world, essentially consists of banks. Although non-bank financial institutions and stock markets have been developing in some African countries, their influence generally remains marginal compared to the banking sector (Brownbridge and Gayi, 1999; Aryeetey, 2004).

In comparative terms, the formal financial sector is performing poorly in Africa. In 2005, the ratio of liquid liabilities (M3) to GDP, an indication of the monetary resources mobilized by the formal financial sector, was 32 per cent in Africa, compared with 49 per cent in East Asia and the Pacific, and 100 per cent in high-income countries (Honohan and Beck, 2007). The comparison is even starker with private sector credit, a key to the intermediary performance of the financial sector. In 2005, private sector credit as a ratio of GDP was 18 per cent in Africa, compared with 30 per cent in South Asia, and 107 per cent in high-income countries (Honohan and Beck, 2007).

Figure 3

Selected indicators of financial depth and financial intermediation

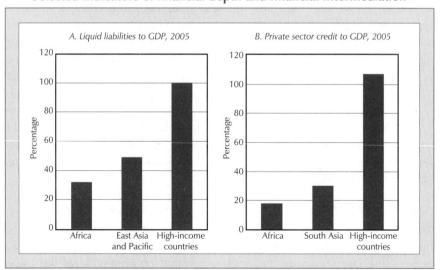

Source: Honohan and Beck, 2007.

Additionally, in Africa banks tend to be concentrated in the principal cities, with few branches in rural areas. Furthermore, they often have rules and procedures for both deposits and loans that prevent poorer households and small businesses from gaining access to their services. Such barriers include minimum deposits and balance for deposits, and high collateral requirements and interest rates for loans. As a result, the banking sector in many African countries is effectively closed off to a large part of the population. In Ghana and the United Republic of Tanzania, for example, only 5 to 6 per cent of the population has access to the banking sector (Basu et al., 2004).

One of the major constraints to the expansion of bank operations in African countries is their limited capacity to manage risk (Nissanke and Aryeetey, 2006). Systemic risks are high in the region, as economies are vulnerable to large externally or internally induced shocks such as terms of trade losses, conflict, extreme climatic events and abrupt policy changes. Honohan and Beck (2007) report that large shocks such as economic or political meltdowns associated with conflict, famine and politico-societal collapse, and external factors occur in sub-Saharan Africa at a rate of one to two per decade per country. Additionally, idiosyncratic risks linked to potential borrowers are also high in the region. There is generally no borrower registry and information on borrowers' risk profiles is difficult if not impossible to obtain, particularly for large centralized banks. Furthermore, contract enforceability is often weak in African countries, making legal recourse against defaulting borrowers an uncertain, lengthy and costly exercise.

The low risk-management capacity of banks in Africa is in large part due to the legacy of pervasive State interventionism in the financial sector. Prior to recent reforms, banks were mostly government-controlled and political imperatives were consistently given priority over commercial viability. Competition between banking institutions remained stifled and banks had little incentive to develop their activities. As a result, the institutional capacity of banks to manage the systemic and idiosyncratic risks in African financial systems has failed to develop sufficiently (Nissanke, 2001).

In part to remedy these problems, many African countries underwent financial sector reforms starting in the mid-1980s. These reforms, which were part of a broader set of market-oriented, often donor-led reforms, generally entailed financial liberalization and institutional reforms to prudential regulation systems and distressed government-owned banks (Brownbridge and Gayi, 1999). They have succeeded in limiting the scope of government intervention in the financial sector and in strengthening prudential regulation of financial institutions. Mostly, however, they have not succeeded in significantly deepening or diversifying the financial sector. In fact, competition has not increased significantly and the banking sector in many countries remains oligopolistic (Senbet and Otchere, 2005). The combination of the low risk-management capacity of banks and the increased emphasis on profitability has induced greater reluctance to take on what are considered costly and risky activities. These include providing banking services to rural households or small informal sector businesses. Banks have therefore closed many of their branches in rural areas and increasingly concentrated their lending on large firms and government bonds. In fact, credit to the private sector as a proportion of GDP decreased in many African countries following the reforms (Steel et al., 1997).

Governments issue bonds at high rates of return in order to attract private funding to cover their fiscal deficits because they no longer have direct access to the resources of the financial sector.[4] These relatively low-risk and high-return assets now make up a significant portion of bank assets. The fact that claims on the private sector represent a significantly lower share of bank assets in Africa, while claims on the Government and State–owned enterprises are higher, suggests that government bonds are crowding out private investment in the region (Honohan and Beck, 2007). Banks in Africa today are largely failing to play their essential role of savings mobilization and financial intermediation. This is evidenced by the fact that despite excess demand for credit, banks often hold high levels of excess liquidity,[5] often in the form of government bonds, and their lending portfolios are dominated by loans to large, often high-risk, private clients (Nissanke and Aryeetey, 2006).

Recently, capital markets have developed considerably in Africa. In 1992, there were 10 stock markets operating in Africa. By 2002, that figure had reached 24 and listed firms numbered 2,216 (Senbet and Otchere, 2005). Nevertheless, African stock markets remain the smallest of any region and are severely illiquid. Of the 15 stock markets in sub-Saharan Africa, seven have market capitalization worth less than 10 per cent of GDP, all except the Johannesburg Stock Exchange have trade values amounting to less than 3 per cent of GDP, and all but three have turnover rates of less than 10 per cent (Honohan and Beck, 2007). This is partly due to the small size of the economies in which they operate. Indeed, it has been found that stock markets appear to emerge and develop only when economies reach a certain size and the level of capital accumulation is high

(Capasso, 2006). It may also be the case that the regulatory requirements imposed on stock markets in the region are unduly high and discourage many firms from using the securities market for raising funds (Honohan and Beck, 2007).

The establishment and relatively good growth performance of African stock markets is nonetheless an encouraging sign. Stock markets can contribute to the deepening and diversification of the financial system and play an important role in risk allocation and risk sharing. It appears, however, that at the current level of development of most African countries, stock markets are unlikely to have a significant impact on the financial system or indeed on economic growth.

The informal financial sector

The informal financial sector refers to all institutions and transactions occurring outside the country's official financial services system. Studies suggest that, in Africa, it is larger than the formal financial sector in terms of influence, coverage and even value of transactions (Nissanke and Aryeetey, 2006). It is estimated that at most only 20 per cent of African households have access to formal finance (Honohan and Beck, 2007).

Institutions offering financial services in the informal sector range from large savings groups to individual moneylenders. The range of services offered is similarly vast, with a large array of different savings collection instruments and lending arrangements, including non-commercial financial transactions between friends and relatives. Some of the most prevalent institutions in this sector are deposit collectors, moneylenders and credit associations. There are also micro-insurance groups that pool small contributions from members and make funds available for particular events such as weddings or funerals (Wright, 1999; Dercon, 2002). Institutions in the informal financial sector typically focus either on deposit collection or on loan extension. The few institutions that offer both services are generally open only to members.

Financial transactions in the informal financial sector are typically small and frequent, reflecting the low level of disposable income and the high liquidity preference of poor households and small businesses. The sector is dynamic, varied and responsive to the needs of the population in terms of financial services. It does not, however, play a significant role in financial intermediation, despite its strong capacity for savings mobilization. It appears that the risk management strategies employed by informal financial institutions, which allow them to operate in the lower end of the financial market, also constrain their expansion.

Informal financial institutions rely on personal relations and repeated transactions as principal risk-reducing strategies. The social pressure exerted by the community in which transactions take place is also of key importance in reducing the likelihood of fraud or default (Nissanke and Aryeetey, 2006). This reliance on personal relations and social pressure constrains the expansion of informal financial institutions beyond the community level. With the advent of new information and communication technologies (ICTs), however, the transaction costs that limit the scale of operations of these institutions should be reduced to a minimum.

Semi-formal financial sector

An important recent phenomenon in African financial systems has been the emergence of microfinance institutions. These are commonly defined as financial institutions dedicated to assisting small enterprises, the poor and households that have no access to the more institutionalized financial system, in mobilizing savings and obtaining access to financial services (Basu et al., 2004). They include institutions from the informal sector as well as a small but growing part of formal financial sector institutions. A number of microfinance institutions, however, fit in neither the informal nor the formal sector. These are institutions that are registered and often regulated to some degree, yet are not treated as banks or subject to the strictest application of prudential regulation.

The emergence of this semi-formal sector holds great potential for bridging the financial services gap that still exists between the informal and formal financial sectors. Many microfinance institutions use the methods and sometimes even the agents of the informal financial sector in providing financial services to poor and rural areas without incurring prohibitive costs. There are also linkages emerging between microfinance institutions and banks as microfinance institutions use large formal banks for deposit and credit facilities.

Semi-formal microfinance institutions deal with risk partly by using agents and methods, such as group-based lending, from the informal financial sector. The main form of risk management, however, is the development of a large client base and the limitation of loan amounts. The portfolio quality of microfinance institutions in Africa is high. It is estimated that the portfolio at risk over 30 days as a proportion of gross loan portfolio is only 4 per cent in Africa, while it is above 5 per cent in East Asia, South Asia and Latin America (Lafourcade et al., 2005).

The strengthening of this semi-formal sector can potentially help deepen and diversify African financial systems. These institutions can play a crucial role in financing small and medium-sized enterprise growth. They can also participate in increasing the mobilization and pooling of financial resources, thereby contributing directly to increasing the amount of domestic resources available for productive investment.

In sum, financial markets remain fragmented and segmented and are not playing their role in the economic development of African countries. Financial intermediation is limited and inefficient in the formal sector, almost non-existent in the informal sector and only emerging in the middle ground between the two. While households have access to some financial services from the informal sector, these remain costly and the resources mobilized are not used for investment purposes. Small and medium-sized firms, meanwhile, are still heavily constrained by their difficulties in accessing financial services that meet their needs, especially in terms of credit. Large formal sector firms and wealthy individuals living in urban centres have less of a problem gaining access to financial services. The resources that banks mobilize, however, tend to be invested in low-risk and high-return government bonds, or lent to "good clients", irrespective of the profitability of the investment (Senbet and Otchere, 2005).

An essential part of enhancing the role of domestic resources in economic development will be increasing the quantity and quality of financial intermediation. Greater integration between the formal and informal financial sectors, possibly through the expansion of the semi-formal sector, would increase the coverage of the financial sector and ensure that the financial needs of more households and firms are met. A more integrated financial sector would be better able to pool mobilized resources and perform essential maturity transformation between volatile savings and stable long-term investments. An efficient financial system with better coverage could raise the level of financial resources in the economy, make a larger proportion of these resources available for investment and improve the allocation of funds for productive investment.

G. Workers' remittances

Remittances, which are monetary or non-monetary resource transfers by migrants to their home countries, are increasingly recognized as an important source of financing for development. They are now the second largest source of capital flows to developing countries, behind FDI but ahead of ODA (Solimano, 2003). As a development resource, remittances have a number of advantages compared with other foreign capital flows. Their stable growth through the growth cycle compares favourably with the volatility of both FDI and ODA flows. They are non-debt-generating and free of conditionalities, and suffer from fewer leakages compared with ODA and FDI. In addition, remittance flows appear to have no negative effects on the export sector of receiving economies (UNECA, 2006).

Data for remittances as reported in International Monetary Fund (IMF) Balance of Payments Statistics fail to accurately measure remittance flows (Solimano, 2003). By including all private transfers to the non-corporate sector, the IMF data tend to include transfers that are not strictly speaking remittances. Nonetheless, as remittances through formal channels are often under-reported, and the large proportion of remittances flowing through informal channels tends to be unreported, it is generally believed that official remittance figures underestimate the actual flows. Official figures do, however, provide an idea of the importance of remittance flows and of their evolution over time.

Officially recorded remittance flows to developing countries have increased from $15 billion in 1980 to $80 billion in 2002, an annual growth rate of 7.7 per cent (Solimano, 2003). Africa as a whole receives around 15 per cent of global remittance flows, with around two thirds of them going to North Africa (UNECA, 2006). Sub-Saharan Africa receives the lowest level of remittances of any region ($4 billion) and records the slowest growth rate of remittances over the 1980–2002 period, with 5.2 per cent (Solimano, 2003). There is, however, reason to believe that official figures for remittances in the region are particularly subject to underestimation as there is a high proportion of remittances flowing through informal channels due to lack of access to formal transfer institutions in many areas.

The fact that much of the migration in the region is intraregional and short to medium term also increases the use of informal channels (Sander and Maimbo, 2003). Additionally, informal transfer agents offer such appealing features as anonymity, speed and minimal paperwork (Gupta et al., 2007). It is therefore estimated that the actual level of remittances in the region is at least twice as high as the reported level (UNECA, 2006).

Figure 4

Capital flows to Africa, 1985–2005

(in US$ millions)

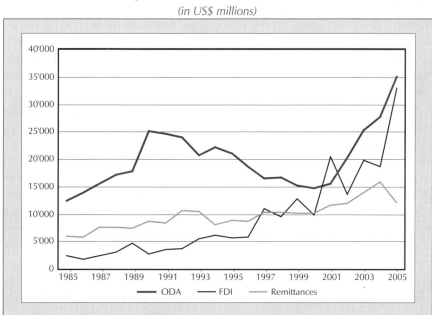

Source: UNCTAD 2006b, OECD 2007 and IMF 2007.

Even the supposedly underestimated figures indicate that remittances at 2.5 per cent of gross national income in 2003 form a significant capital inflow to African countries. However, the importance of remittances varies hugely from country to country. Egypt, Gambia, Lesotho and Morocco all receive remittances worth over 5 per cent of their gross national income, but remittances are negligible in many other countries.

The level of remittance flows to or from a country is essentially driven by the prevailing patterns of migration. More emigrants with higher levels of education and commanding higher wages in their countries of residence will generate higher remittance inflows. Obviously, the benefit of remittances, while important, can at best mitigate only a small part of the cost to the country of people emigrating in the first place. This cost is especially high in sub-Saharan Africa, as skilled emigration is particularly high. Some countries, such as Burundi or Mozambique, have lost over a third of their educated workforce to emigration (Gupta et al., 2007).

With regard to the motivations of migrants sending remittances, the distinction is generally made between altruistic motives and self-interested motives. The altruistic motive relates to migrants sending remittances back home in order to improve the well-being of relatives in their home countries. In contrast, the self-interested motive relates to a portfolio choice on the part of the migrant to invest in assets in his home country. If the altruistic motive predominates, remittance inflows could be expected to be counter-cyclical. Conversely, if the selfish motive is stronger, remittance inflows would likely be pro-cyclical. In fact, empirical evidence is unclear and it would seem that remittance inflows reflect both types of motivation, with remittances to sub-Saharan Africa showing remarkable stability throughout the growth cycle (Gupta et al., 2007).

Remittances can have a positive impact on receiving countries in a number of ways. Firstly, as inflows of foreign capital, remittances improve the balance of payments situation of receiving countries. Secondly, remittances directly reduce poverty and help households smooth their consumption patterns, thereby indirectly contributing to stabilizing the country's economic activity (UNDP, 2005). It is estimated that around 80 per cent of remittances in Africa are used for consumption and schooling (UNECA, 2006). Consumption increases demand for local products and through indirect multiplier effects can promote employment and investment. Spending on schooling or health meanwhile improves the human capital of the country, thereby influencing its productivity. Investment in land, livestock or real estate is also common, though secondary to daily needs and human capital expenses (Sander and Maimbo, 2003). Finally, there is some evidence of remittances being increasingly used for investment purposes, mainly in financing small and medium-sized enterprises or small infrastructure projects (Sander and Maimbo, 2003; UNDP, 2005).

In sum, remittances are an important and steadily growing resource for development, and help offset the costs of emigration, increase households' incomes and ameliorate receiving countries' external balance. With the appropriate policies and institutions in place, they could be better harnessed as a development resource and channelled into productive investment, thereby contributing to employment and growth.

H. Capital flight

Capital flight reduces the amount of resources available for domestic investment, both private and public. Understanding the determinants of capital flight in order to reduce its magnitude can therefore contribute to increasing the level of domestic savings and investment.

Capital flight is not a clearly defined concept, and different definitions and measurements exist. The essential conceptual difference between various measures for capital flight lies in the coverage of outflows of capital, particularly whether the distinction is made between capital flight caused by political and economic uncertainty, and "normal" capital outflows that would happen regardless of such uncertainties. Thus, while one set of measures looks at the total amount of resources leaving the country, the other looks more specifically at episodic surges of capital "fleeing" unfavourable conditions. Understandably, these different sets of measures produce conflicting estimations of the magnitude of capital flight in African countries. Indeed, there are not many empirical studies of capital flight in African countries and differences in capital flight definitions, calculation methods, sample countries and years covered make comparisons between these studies almost impossible.

Highly conservative estimates of capital flight from Africa suggest that it averaged nearly $3 billion per year between 1976 and 1997, an annual loss of 2.6 per cent of GDP (Lensink et al., 2000). Other estimates report capital flight levels of above $13 billion per year between 1991 and 2004, a staggering 7.6 per cent of annual GDP (Salisu, 2005). It has been estimated that the cumulative stock of flight capital for sub-Saharan Africa from 1970 to 1996 was approximately $285 billion. Considering that the combined external debt of the region was $178 billion as of 1996, this arguably makes sub-Saharan Africa a "net creditor" vis-à-vis the rest of the world (Boyce and Ndikumana, 2001).

Just as there are important differences between estimates of the magnitude of capital flight from African countries, there is no consensus on their evolution over time. Indeed, while Collier, Hoeffler and Patillo (2004) suggest that capital flight peaked at 35 per cent of private sector wealth in 1988 and has since been declining, Salisu (2005) estimates that capital flight doubled from $15 billion in 1991 to $30 billion in 2003.

What emerges from all these studies is that capital flight is currently diverting a large amount of resources from countries that are in urgent need of financing for development. In effect, whether the magnitude of capital flight is 5 per cent of GDP (Ajayi, 1997) or more than 7 per cent (Salisu, 2005), it is clear that reversing a large part of the flight could greatly reduce the resource gap in African countries.

Capital flight is the result of a decision to hold assets abroad rather than within the domestic economy. As such, it is responsive to factors such as macroeconomic and political instability, as well as financial market depth, all of which influence the risk-adjusted returns of domestic assets.

Empirical studies that have sought to determine more precisely which factors most affect the level of capital flight yield different results according to the definition of capital flight and the sample choice. However, some factors appear to be more influential than others. Among indicators of financial instability, the level of external debt appears to be the most clearly correlated to capital flight. It seems that debt serves as a signal both of economic mismanagement and of future increases in taxation, therefore instigating capital flight. There is also evidence that in some cases debt has provided the funds for capital flight (Ajayi, 1997). Other indicators of economic mismanagement also seem to influence capital flight. These include currency overvaluation, fiscal imbalances and high inflation rates. The empirical evidence regarding their influence over capital flight rates in Africa is, however, more ambiguous.

Political stability has a strong influence on capital flight. It directly induces greater capital flight and often leads to macroeconomic instability, thus reducing investment opportunities and increasing the risk associated with holding domestic assets. Indicators of political stability and good governance are therefore negatively related to rates of capital flight (Collier et al., 2004; Lensink et al., 2000).

Differences in the rate of growth between two economies also promote capital flight from the slower growing economy to the faster growing one, reflecting increased opportunities and better returns. Levels of financial deepening are also expected to reduce the incentive for capital flight by increasing the quantity and quality of domestic investment opportunities as well as the returns on such investments (UNECA, 2006). The effect of capital account liberalization, which has been a component of financial sector reforms in many African countries, on capital flight is contested. While liberalization makes it easier to transfer assets abroad, whether legally or illegally, it has also been argued that it creates investment opportunities domestically. The empirical evidence on the subject is mixed (Collier et al., 2001).

Capital flight, however defined, currently denies African countries a considerable amount of resources. Its reversal could contribute to filling the resource gap in African countries.

I. Conclusion

Domestic financial resources in Africa are mainly drawn from private savings and government revenue. Gross domestic saving rates are low and unstable in Africa, and they have fallen considerably over the past four decades. Paradoxically, research suggests that African households do save a considerable proportion of their income. However, in large part due to the weakness of the formal financial sector, these savings take place in non-financial form or in the informal sector, where they are not intermediated towards productive investment. Firms also generate savings, but the ill-functioning credit market forces them to retain their earnings principally for self-investment.

Tax revenues are relatively low in most of sub-Saharan Africa, partly reflecting administrative and technical difficulties in tax collection. In many countries in Africa, raising additional tax revenue is further constrained by weak State legitimacy, as taxes have often not translated into improvements in public service delivery. Thus, there is a danger of depressing economic activity if taxes are pushed higher without a corresponding increase in State legitimacy. Much can be done, however, in terms of improving the quality of public expenditure and investment, as is discussed in chapter 2.

The financial system has an essential role to play both in terms of improving domestic resource mobilization and in channelling those resources towards productive investments. At present, however, its performance in both these aspects is poor. The formal financial sector caters almost exclusively to the needs of a small, urban-based elite of formal firms, wealthy individuals and Governments. The informal financial sector meanwhile provides financial services to poor households, but the resources thus mobilized are not intermediated towards productive investments. There are nonetheless some encouraging signs of an emerging semi-formal sector that may be able to respond to the financial needs of small and medium-sized enterprises in some countries. Advances in technology may also help to improve the provision of financial services. Mobile phone banking, for example, allows banks to offer their services to a broad base of customers at reduced cost.

Workers' remittances are an important capital flow which has been steadily increasing in volume over the years. Their exact magnitude is not known, as a large portion of remittances in Africa is thought to be transmitted through informal channels. Remittances contribute to the receiving households' finances and are mainly used for basic needs and education.

Capital flight reduces the amount of domestic resources available for productive investment within a country. Though definitions and estimations differ, it is clear that capital flight remains a severe drain on domestic resources in several African countries, and that a reversal of this flight would likely have a great impact on the availability of domestic resources for development.

The low productivity of investment and high level of liquidity in banks in Africa suggest that the availability of domestic resources is only one side of the equation. Maximizing the development impact of such resources will require much greater attention to increasing both their volume and their use. Improving the mobilization and use of domestic resources should have a strong positive impact on development in African countries. Increased levels of domestic resources and the corresponding decrease in dependence on aid should enable them to increase their "ownership" of the development process, and identify priority sectors for investment that generate sustained growth within the context of a developmental State.

Chapter 2

THE CHALLENGE OF INCREASING SAVINGS AND BOOSTING PRODUCTIVE INVESTMENT

A. Introduction

Achieving high and sustainable levels of investment needed for Africa's development will require a more balanced combination of foreign and domestic resources than has been the case until now. It is expected that more reliance on domestic resources will give countries more policy space to implement strategies that reflect their development priorities, unlike past strategies, which were donor driven. After all, African leaders are answerable to Africans, albeit imperfectly, but donors are not. The resulting increase in ownership of the development agenda should boost the efficiency of development strategies if they focus on those sectors where investment is most productive.

Realistically, boosting domestic savings will require higher rates of economic growth sustained over a long period. ODA could trigger this growth process if it focused on financing pro-growth public investment such as economic infrastructure. Such investment would in turn crowd in domestically financed private investment.[6] The higher growth rates resulting from these investments would eventually generate more domestic resources and more investment, sustaining high growth rates, and so on. Once set in motion, this virtuous circle is possible even though Africans are thought to be too poor to save. After all, poor countries in East Asia and other developing regions have been able to save, invest and grow.

The relationship between savings and investment shows a mixed picture. In the long term, the correlation between savings and investment rates is positive and strong. From 1960 to 2005, the correlation coefficient between gross capital formation and gross domestic savings was 0.74. In the short term, however, there is almost no relationship between these two variables. In 2005, for example, the cross-country correlation coefficient stood at only 0.05. Indeed, country comparisons show that the countries with the highest investment rates are not necessarily the ones with high savings rates. Sao Tome and Principe had the highest rate of gross capital formation, representing 44 per cent of GDP, but the second-lowest rate of gross domestic savings, representing –26.4 per cent of GDP. Some of the highest investment rates in 2005 were recorded in countries with the lowest savings rates. Zimbabwe, Lesotho, Ethiopia and Rwanda had investment rates ranging from 38 per cent to 21 per cent of GDP against savings rates of 3 per cent to –11 per cent of GDP (World Bank, 2007a).

One possible explanation of these contrasting results is that short-term investments are strongly affected by external sources, particularly ODA, while in the long term, investments are determined more by domestic savings. Indeed, despite the positive role played by foreign aid in Africa's development, overdependence on ODA to fund domestic investments raises some issues. Firstly, such investments are difficult to predict and sustain, given the high volatility of ODA. Indeed, ODA to Africa has been found to be up to four times more volatile than government revenue (UNCTAD, 2006a). Secondly, increases in aid to specific countries have not usually been sustained for more than a few years. Thirdly, the decision about which sectors to invest in may reflect donor rather than national interests. The experience of aid conditionality in the current poverty reduction strategy papers illustrates this point clearly (see UNCTAD, 2002, 2006a).[7] There is general consensus that Governments should fully own their development programmes. Such "ownership" is difficult when the implementation of the development programme is largely dependent on external sources of finance, particularly when donors' priorities do not coincide with those of the recipient countries. Fourthly, aid cannot directly finance private sector investment, which is the type of investment most needed to sustain rapid growth in Africa. Furthermore, even when investment rates are high, efficiency of such investments is sometimes low, reducing their potential positive effect on economic growth (see chapter 3).

B. Increasing savings

In the light of the discussion in chapter 1 on the determinants of savings, five propositions are explored in order to offer possible ways of increasing savings in Africa: (a) controlling demographic factors; (b) financial sector reforms and development of the informal financial sector; (c) increasing investment opportunities; (d) reducing capital flight and inefficiencies in resource allocation; and (e) reforming the tax sector.

Controlling demographic factors

Africa is the only region of the world that has not achieved a demographic transition (UNECA, 2005c). It has been argued that Africa's high fertility rates[8] have kept its dependency ratios very high.[9] It is however, generally acknowledged that high dependency ratios make savings difficult. As income is shared among several people, very little is left for saving, particularly when household incomes are relatively low. Therefore, for domestic savings to increase, the dependency ratio should decline, per capita income should increase, or both. Decreasing the dependency ratio is difficult in the short term. However, there are positive signs that Africa may succeed in reducing its dependency ratio, as the continent's annual population growth rate is expected to decline from the current 2.5 per cent to 2 per cent over the next 10 years (McKinley, 2005). Moreover, if the relatively high economic growth rates achieved in Africa the last few years are sustained, these rates, in combination with low population growth, could induce higher savings rates.

These positive changes need to be balanced against the negative effect of pandemics such as HIV/AIDS, malaria and tuberculosis on African countries' capacity to save. These pandemics are destroying human capital at a rate never experienced before. In some countries, particularly in Southern Africa, the rate of attrition of professionals such as teachers, health workers, construction workers and mineworkers is so fast that they cannot be replaced fast enough (UNECA, 2005c). In the absence of reliable social security systems, a growing number of survivors are also using their resources, including their savings and time, to provide care to the sick and orphans. As a result, these pandemics have dented Africa's meager financial and human resources, leading to even lower savings rates.

Financial sector reforms and development of the informal financial sector

Financial sector reforms carried out in Africa in the 1990s have had a limited impact on domestic resource mobilization, as chapter 1 has shown. The traditional concentration of the banking sector on import–export activities to the detriment of productive investment in agriculture and industry has not changed. Moreover, commercial banks are still concentrating their activities on large clients, such as large firms in the private sector, as well as the public sector. Furthermore, the fact that those banks have traditionally shied away from the rural economy in Africa, where most productive activities are located, suggests that important savings remain untapped. Indeed, the formal financial sector has not adapted to the reality of the post-colonial State, where small and medium-sized enterprises dominate the economy. As Steel et al. (1997) put it, formal banks have little interest and experience in serving small clients, particularly in rural areas. Therefore, informal financial institutions should be empowered to monetize and mobilize domestic savings, as they are more appropriately adapted to developing countries' financial needs.

There is some evidence that, although they had no important effect on formal financial institutions, financial reforms remarkably increased the performance of informal financial institutions (Steel et al., 1997). Survey evidence shows that between 1990 and 1992 in the United Republic of Tanzania, the volume of deposits in savings and credit cooperatives increased by 67 per cent, while deposits in rotating savings and credit associations increased by 113 per cent, thanks to higher numbers of clients and larger average savings.[10]

Similar trends were observed in Nigeria over the same period. Deposits in savings and credit associations rose by 56 per cent and those of rotating savings and credit associations by 77 per cent, while the capital base of savings and loan companies grew by 148 per cent (Steel et al., 1997). In Burundi, although microfinance is a relatively new phenomenon, its activities have increased substantially over the last decade. Unlike the formal banking sector, microfinance institutions are present in almost all of the country's 116 administrative communes. In 2005, the registered microfinance institutions had 300,000 members, or about 5 per cent of the population. They mobilized $14 million and there is potential for further expansion (Nzobonimpa et al., 2006).

Despite its relevance and impressive growth, the microfinance sector by itself cannot fill the current intermediation deficiencies. Microfinance institutions have the advantage of covering a large number of small savers in areas where formal banks are absent but the amounts involved in each operation are relatively small, as the evidence from Burundi has shown. Moreover, as already suggested, microfinance institutions are able to cover only a small fraction of the total demand for financial services. The reasons for the limited expansion of microfinance institutions and their inability to fill the intermediation gaps include: (a) lack of stable resources, obliging the institutions to lend only in the short term; (b) lack of human and technical capacity of the lenders and borrowers to manage larger volumes of operations and design large investment projects; and

(c) the high cost of credit due to high interest rates paid to commercial banks, which provide the advances that microfinance institutions turn into loans to members (see Nzobonimpa et al., 2006).

The message here is that even if microfinance institutions currently mobilize relatively small amounts, they are able to provide financial services to segments that the formal banking sector cannot reach. Moreover, the steady increase of microfinance institutions over the years, particularly in comparison to the formal banking sector, suggests that they have the potential to widen their services to more clients traditionally outside the credit market. Hence, given their respective roles, the formal banking sector and microfinance provide complementary credit delivery mechanisms. Strengthening the synergies between these two types of institutions would increase the quality and quantity of services provided to the public. Chapter 4 proposes some specific strategies that could be used to mobilize more stable domestic long-term financial resources.

Increasing investment opportunities

Mainstream economists argue that the low rates of investment in developing countries are primarily due to low savings. While this is true to some extent, Keynesian economists point to the possibility of reverse causality, from low investment to low savings due to the multiplier and accelerator effects.[11] As discussed earlier, the initial investment, funded by external resources, would then create its own savings through the multiplier effect.

However, the mismatch in the term structure between savings (short-term) and productive investments (long-term) implies that many countries have problems transforming savings into productive investment, as illustrated by large excess liquidity in the banking sector. A 2003 study of the banking sector in the Central Africa region found that commercial banks maintained high liquidity ratios. Liquidity ratios of banks in Cameroon, Chad and Equatorial Guinea were higher than 200 per cent, while the ratios for Gabon and the Central African Republic were 183 per cent and 101 per cent, respectively (Avom and Eyeffa, 2006). A similar situation was observed in Ghana, Malawi, Nigeria and the United Republic of Tanzania in the 1990s (Steel et al., 1997) and Burundi in 2005 (Nzobonimpa et al., 2006).

As a result, only a small proportion of savings is allocated to long-term credit that finances productive investment. In Burundi, for example, long-term credit (more than five years of maturity) represented only 3 per cent of total credit in 2004, compared with 17 per cent and 80 per cent for medium-term (one to five years) and short-term (less than one year) credit, respectively. Although this term structure is not particular to Africa, the absence of sophisticated bond markets in the continent to provide reliable long-term savings and borrowing instruments that limit the amount of long-term investible funds, create what has been termed "original sin" facing most developing economies.[12] Used in a way that preserves a country's domestic debt sustainability, bond markets not only allow Governments to borrow in order to invest in long-term investment projects, such as infrastructure, they also provide banks with an opportunity for portfolio diversification.[13] Therefore, the promotion of capital markets could attenuate the problems due to the unavailability of long-term credit affecting most countries in Africa.

Reducing capital flight and inefficiencies in resource allocation

The discussion in chapter 1 highlighted the extent to which capital flight robs Africa of its much-needed financial resources. If these resources could be efficiently invested within the continent, African countries could raise their domestic savings remarkably. Capital flight is both a cause and a consequence of a country's poor investment performance. In the current context of high capital mobility, capital flight may be a rational response to the lack of profitable investment opportunities within Africa. Moreover, Boyce and Ndikumana (2001), show that capital flight is intimately associated with a country's external debt. In this regard, debt relief could reduce capital flight and increase domestic savings, particularly if complementary improvements in governance are made to ensure that countries do not fall back into the debt trap.

Political and economic governance are also important determinants of capital flight. Those involved in capital flight are usually Africa's political and economic elites, who are engaged in illegal practices to appropriate their countries' wealth. They use a variety of means, including trade misinvoicing; embezzlement of tax revenue, exports and aid; and kickbacks on contracts. These practices result in a skewed distribution of wealth within the society. On the one hand are members of the elite who engage in capital flight and lavish spending rather than saving and investing in their economies. On the other hand are poor people who have to struggle to make ends meet. The result is a high level of income inequality, illustrated by the fact that Africa has the world's second-highest Gini coefficient (42) after only Latin America (50).[14] It is not by coincidence that countries such as Nigeria, South Africa and Zambia have a combination of some of the highest levels of inequality and capital flight. These two issues are not just economic; they have a governance dimension that needs to be addressed appropriately.

Inefficient spending is another channel through which African economies are starved of the resources needed for productive investment. As it is difficult to find a good measure of waste in the way resources are used, total factor productivity growth could be used as a proxy measure of the efficiency with which resources are used. Results based on macroeconomic accounting have found that from 1960 to 2000, average total factor productivity growth in Africa declined from a relatively high value of 2 per cent per annum in the 1960s (the same as the world average) to negative values in the 1970–2000 period (Collins and Bosworth, 2003). As a result, annual growth of output per worker in Africa grew by only 0.6 per cent over the period, well below the world average of 2.3 per cent.

Although there are no statistics to support the argument that low total factor productivity growth in Africa was due, at least partly, to allocative inefficiencies or wasteful spending, political economy considerations could help explain why resources are not optimally used. As noted in the case of capital flight discussed above (see also the discussions in chapter 3), there have been instances where state and private assets were appropriated by ruling elites who used them for their own benefit. Collier and O'Connell (2007) use 26 detailed case studies of growth in Africa over the period 1960–2000 to show, among other things, how inefficient redistributions were associated with allocative inefficiencies. The improvement in governance across the continent as illustrated by the adoption of the African Peer Review Mechanism (see chapter 3 for details) has already reduced the effect of many of these negative factors and improved the overall image of the continent.

African leaders did not make these policy choices with the intention of destroying their economies. In some instances, decisions that turned out later to be inefficacious were made with the genuine belief that they would lead countries to a path of growth and development (e.g. United Republic of Tanzania President Julius Nyerere's "African Socialism" or Ujamaa). One should also add that these policies reflected the development paradigm at the time, and were even supported by multilateral financial institutions (Mbabazi and Taylor, 2005: 7–8). Some other decisions, however, reflect institutional weaknesses that failed to force some leaders to behave responsibly in the interest of the majority.

This was the case with some redistribution policies. These weaknesses require modern and strong economic and political institutions that should outline the rules defining the boundaries within which political leaders make their choices. In other words, the State must be empowered to fully play its role in a context of clearly defined obligations and prerogatives.

Reforming the tax sector

One area of economic governance that needs attention is the administration of the tax system, considering that most Governments derive much of their domestic revenue from taxation. If taxes were efficiently collected and embezzlement tackled, tax revenue should increase substantially (Fjeldstad and Semboja, 2001). Although the reason for uncollected taxes is partly due to inefficiencies and limited administrative capacity, tax collectors often collude with taxpayers in many countries to defraud the State of part of its revenue (Fjeldstad, 2005).

A number of countries in Africa have changed their tax policies, sometimes under pressure from their development partners. Initially, these reforms had some success, as the Ugandan experience showed. The reforms helped create tax systems that are more income elastic, more broadly based and less distorting to economic activity. However, since it is much easier to change policies than to change institutions, tax administration is still a major problem. Taxpayers do not believe that their taxes are properly used to produce the expected basic services the State should provide. As discussed in chapter 1, this reduces their incentive to pay taxes, which could explain, at least partly, why tax policy reforms have so far had limited effects (see Fjeldstad and Semboja, 2001).

Policies aimed at increasing government revenue through greater tax compliance must balance three pillars. Firstly, the State must be legitimate with a clear contract with taxpayers, where the obligations of the State towards taxpayers are respected. For example, if the State invests the tax collected into public and social services that benefit the community, taxpayers would be less likely to engage in tax evasion as a form of protest against predatory authorities. Secondly, tax collection entails some form of coercion. If it were left to each individual to decide whether to pay taxes, opportunistic tax avoidance would probably be rampant. Taxes are transfers from the fruit of individual or company efforts to other entities, so it is the element of coercion that distinguishes them from philanthropic donations. Thirdly, it is important to put in place a reliable mechanism of detecting and punishing tax evaders. Coercion would become meaningless if tax evaders could not be detected and appropriately punished. These three elements must be taken together. The relatively low tax compliance in Africa seems to be due to the fact that countries have a tendency to put more emphasis on the second pillar of the policy, without giving due regard to the first and third pillars (Fjeldstad and Semboja, 2001).

C. Credit constraints

Credit is the main channel through which savings are transformed into investments. Not all savings are used to finance investment, despite high demand for credit, because the credit market in Africa is rationed. Indeed, the lack of credit has been cited by firm managers in Africa as their most important constraint (Bigsten and Soderbom, 2005). Access to credit is important because it affects the level of investment made by a firm, which in turn is associated with its growth and overall contribution to economic activity. Credit constraints also affect the efficiency of investment (Bigsten et al., 1999). The lack of the required amounts of credit can force a firm to postpone, scale down or even abandon investment plans that are crucial for its economic viability, thus affecting the firm's profitability and growth. Moreover, financially constrained firms are less able to adjust to short-term shocks to their cash flow, which could impair their activities.

Recent studies have shown that the borrowing of firms from the banking sector is very low in Africa. Based on a sample of manufacturing firms in Burundi, Cameroon, Côte d'Ivoire, Ghana, Kenya and Zimbabwe, Bigsten et al. (2003) found that 55 per cent of the firms did not apply for loans; 33 per cent were in need of loans but their applications were rejected; and 12 per cent of the firms received loans. Of course, the fact that a firm does not finance its activities with a loan is not necessarily due to credit rationing, because some firms may not have the need for credit. Credit rationed firms are those that apply for loans and have their applications rejected, or those that do not apply because they believe their applications would be rejected. As these figures show, a third of the firms in the sample are credit rationed.

The same study found that the rate of credit rationing decreases as firm size increases. For example, 64 per cent of firms with less than five workers and 42 per cent of firms with six to 25 workers are credit rationed. However, only 10 per cent of firms with more than 100 workers are credit rationed. About two-thirds of the large firms do not participate in the credit market because they use their retained profits. Considering that African economies are dominated by small firms without adequate resources of their own, credit rationing is a critical problem.

Why are so many firms and households unable to access credit even when the banks have excess liquidity? Two major factors limit firms and households' access to finance. Firstly, transaction costs associated with credit delivery to small customers are high, particularly where large numbers of credit applicants live in remote areas. The basic infrastructure essential for an efficient running of banking operations is often lacking in rural areas, preventing formal banks from penetrating this segment of the credit market. For example, it is inconceivable for a bank to open branches in areas lacking key services such as access roads, electricity or telephones,[15] which are too costly to provide privately to an atomized rural market. Secondly, information asymmetries between banks and borrowers are high due to the absence of credit information systems. As a result, banks are discouraged from extending their credit market because of the difficulty of determining the true creditworthiness of borrowers and the high cost of enforcing credit contracts once lending has taken place (Honohan and Beck, 2007).

High transaction costs

In most African countries, the oldest banks are financial institutions inherited from the colonial period. These banks are often subsidiaries of metropolitan parent banks, and their focus is on financing international trade and the services sector, because these sectors provide quick high returns. Data collected in 2001 show that in Botswana, Guinea–Bissau and Lesotho, all banking assets were owned by foreign banks. In addition, at least two thirds of banking assets were owned by foreign banks in Benin, Côte d'Ivoire, Gambia, Guinea, Madagascar, Mali, Namibia, Niger, Senegal and Swaziland (World Bank, 2007a).[16] These banks lend to larger borrowers such as the public sector, large enterprises and wealthy households. They do not have mechanisms well suited to catering to the needs of small, low-income and mostly agricultural and rural-based economic agents, despite the fact that these agents constitute the backbone of African economies. Instead, small borrowers have heavily relied on the informal financial sector. Financial liberalization of the 1990s had little effect on this financial market fragmentation.

In contrast, microfinance institutions operate with minimum infrastructure, making them more efficient in rural credit markets. Unfortunately, whereas formal banks have excess liquidity, microcredit institutions have limited resources, constraining their financial and geographic coverage. It is estimated that microfinance institutions in Burundi were able to extend credit amounting to about $16 million in 2005, satisfying only 30 per cent of the demand (Nzobonimpa et al., 2006). Although it appears small, this coverage is much higher than the rate of successful applications in the traditional banking sector reported by Bigsten et al. (2003) for Burundi, Cameroon, Côte d'Ivoire, Ghana, Kenya and Zimbabwe. Only 3 per cent of micro firms and 8 per cent of small-scale firms applied for and received credit. In addition, the estimated amount of credit needed by those using microfinance institutions is 40 per cent higher than total equity of all the country's commercial and development banks. Hence, those with relatively large investment projects cannot rely on microfinance to meet their needs.

The second aspect of transaction costs incurred by formal banks relates to their high administrative costs, which include the costs of screening, monitoring and contract enforcement. In their study of the informal financial sector in African countries in the early 1990s, Steel et al. (1997) find that traditional commercial and development banks incur loan administrative costs that could be more than 10 times higher than microfinance institutions.[17] Administrative costs of loans to small-scale enterprises by commercial and development banks in Nigeria and the United Republic of Tanzania represented 13 per cent and 12 per cent of the loans, respectively. Comparatively, the costs were 1.9 per cent and 2.5 per cent for credit unions in Nigeria and the United Republic of Tanzania, 1 per cent and 0.1 per cent for savings and credit cooperatives, respectively. Urban moneylenders' administrative costs amounted to 3.2 per cent and 1.7 per cent in Nigeria and the United Republic of Tanzania, respectively.

The foregoing shows that the financial market is segmented: the formal banking sector focuses on large customers, whereas the informal sector specializes in collecting savings from and lending to small customers. According to Bigsten et al. (2003), a bank requires a profit to capital ratio of 200 per cent to grant a loan to a firm with less than five permanent workers, all else being equal, because it is too difficult and risky to deal with these small firms. The ratio drops to 56 per cent if the firm has between 26 and 100 workers. Given the dominance of small firms in African economies, appropriate measures should be put in place to address their financial needs. For example, commercial banks' excess liquidity could be efficiently used if there were proper channels through which they could reach small and medium-sized enterprises that are in need. Allowing communication between these two segments would be one way of reducing the level of credit rationing affecting small firms.

Some countries have recently encouraged such communication through the creation of semi-formal financial institutions or the establishment in commercial banks of special windows dedicated to small borrowers. In South Africa, the enactment of the Usury Act Exemption Notice in 1999 induced banks to create their own micro-lending subsidiaries, which cater to the specific needs of small borrowers previously kept outside the credit market.[18] By 2002, these subsidiaries accounted for almost half of the $2 billion owed to formal microcredit institutions (Meagher and Wilkinson, 2002). In Central and West Africa, ECOBANK, a regional commercial bank operating in 13 countries, has recently established special windows dedicated to small and medium-sized enterprises.

Limited credit information

Credit trade in Africa is seriously handicapped by the lack of reasonable credit information[19] coverage, whether by private bureaus or public registries. The only countries with good coverage of private bureaus are South Africa, where the coverage rate in 2006 was 53 per cent of the adult population; Botswana with 43 per cent; Swaziland with 39 per cent; and Namibia with 35 per cent. Public registries have some importance in Cape Verde and Tunisia, each with 12 per cent of adults covered, followed by Benin and Mauritius, with 10 per cent each. Sub-Saharan Africa has the second-lowest rate of private bureau coverage in the world. On average, only 3.6 per cent of the adult population is covered, in comparison to 60.8 per cent for OECD countries (World Bank, 2007c).

In the absence of credit information, banks tend to "personalize" credit, concentrating their lending on a small group of clients who have developed a reputation for creditworthiness through past interactions. Indeed, one of the most interesting results emanating from the econometric literature on the determinants of bank credit supply in Africa is that banks tend to lend to the firms that are already in debt. The reason is that known creditworthy borrowers are so few that banks compete to lend to them even before they finish paying their previous debts. As a result, being in debt signals creditworthiness rather than a high risk of default. However, the relationship between debt and access to credit is an inverted u-shape, implying a level of debt beyond which banks are reluctant to provide more loans. Using econometric results in Bigsten et al. (2003) where other determinants of credit are controlled for, this threshold can be situated approximately at the level where debt represents 60 per cent of a firm's capital.

Ensuring creditworthiness ex ante is very important because collateral is not a good protection against default. Because credit contracts are not properly enforced, it is extremely difficult to seize and sell the collateral of a defaulting borrower. A project with a high expected profitability rate signals the capacity but not necessarily the willingness of the credit applicant to service his debt. In this regard, credit contracts are implicitly based on the reputation of the borrower, not on the value of collateral. The exceptionally high levels of collateral (up to six times the amount of the loan) are used to indicate compliance with banking regulations concerning portfolio risk profile (Nkurunziza, 2005b).

From the discussion above, two important policy conclusions emerge. Firstly, financial policy reforms should acknowledge the existence and usefulness of a segmented credit market and the important role played by microfinance. What is thus needed is to put in place measures to create more synergies between microfinance and the formal banking sector. Secondly, putting in place credit information infrastructure and developing a legal system that enforces credit contracts should be the two pillars of a new agenda for financial sector reforms.

An important caveat should be kept in mind in the discussion of credit policies. Survey evidence shows that a large number of firms do not borrow, either because they do not need credit or because they do not have the capacity to repay. Extending credit across the board could harm such firms. For example, an econometric study on the effect of credit on firm survival in Kenya's manufacturing sector in the 1990s, a period of economic turbulence, found that firms using credit increased their odds of collapse by 92 per cent relative to firms not using credit (Nkurunziza, 2005a). This was because these firms were facing several other problems that eroded their capacities to use credit profitably. Therefore, although the lack of access to credit is an important problem, it is just one of many challenges facing firms in Africa.

D. Barriers to investment in Africa

High risk and a generally poor business environment are key determinants of low investment rates in Africa. Due to credit rationing and high investment risk, many economies in Africa are caught in a low-level "equilibrium of low demand and low supply of credit" (Nzobonimpa et al., 2006: 17). As a result, firms' decisions to invest are highly correlated with profitability. However, very high profit rates are needed to convince an entrepreneur to make even some small investments. For example, evidence based on survey data on manufacturing firms in Cameroon, Ghana, Kenya and Zimbabwe shows that the firms that invest are those with high profit rates, suggesting that firms rely on retaining earnings to fund investment. However, due to the high risk prevailing in those economies, only between 6 to 10 per cent of profits is invested (Bigsten et al., 2003). The discussion in this section focuses on five main barriers to investment, one structural and four institutional: (a) poor infrastructure, (b) high entry costs, (c) labour market constraints, (d) low investor protection, and (e) high taxes and a cumbersome tax system.[20] Initial investment takes place when its risk-adjusted expected benefits outweigh the costs. Table 2 gives a comparative view of business costs in Africa relative to other regions.

Table 2
Regional comparative data on the cost of doing business

Region	Starting business (% GNI per cap.)	Licences cost (% per cap. inc.)	Non-wage labour cost (% salary)	Credit informa- tion index	Investor protection index	Total tax rate (% profit)	Import cost ($ per container)	Export cost ($ per container)	Enforcing contracts (% debt)
East Asia & Pacific	42.8	207.2	9.4	1.9	5.2	42.2	1,037.1	884.8	52.7
Europe & Central Asia	14.1	564.9	26.7	2.9	4.8	56.0	1,589.3	1,450.2	15.0
Latin America & Caribbean	48.1	246.2	12.5	3.4	5.1	49.1	1,225.5	1,067.5	23.4
Middle East & North Africa	74.5	499.9	15.6	2.4	4.6	40.8	1,182.8	923.9	17.7
OECD	5.3	72.0	21.4	5.0	6.0	47.8	882.6	811.0	11.2
South Asia	46.6	375.7	6.8	1.8	5.0	45.1	1,494.9	1,236.0	26.4
Sub-Saharan Africa	**162.8**	**1,024.5**	**12.7**	**1.3**	**4.7**	**71.2**	**1,946.9**	**1,561.1**	**42.2**

Source: World Bank (2007a).

Notes: **Credit information index:** ranges from zero to 6; high values mean more information availability. **Investor protection index:** ranges from zero to 10; higher values mean better protection. Measurement units of other variables are explained in their respective headings.

Poor infrastructure

Poor infrastructure in many African countries discourages investment because it increases production costs. This is the case with international transport costs, defined here as the costs of moving goods between countries. As table 2 shows, import and export costs are highest in Africa. On average, they represent 11 per cent of the value of imports, compared with 7 per cent in Latin America and the Caribbean, and 8 per cent in Asia. In landlocked African countries, transport costs represent 19 per cent of import value (UNCTAD, 1999). These high costs particularly inflate the cost of production of manufactured goods with a high content of imported inputs. High international transport costs also increase export costs, reducing exporters' profit rates. As a result, high transport costs have a significant effect on the location of foreign investors.

There is so far little microeconomic evidence on the impact of domestic infrastructure on firm investment. However, opinion surveys of firm managers in Africa report that poor infrastructure is the third-leading constraint to investment, the other two being financing and corruption (Bigsten and Soderbom, 2005). As explained earlier, the availability and reliability of basic infrastructure such as access roads, electricity and telephones is essential to major investments, so their absence or unreliability precludes such investments. In a number of African countries, firms are obliged to invest in electricity generation by buying their own generators, due to the unreliability of the national electricity grid. This imposes a high cost and reduces the resources that could have been invested on other productive activities. In many cases, potential investments are not made due to the absence of basic infrastructure, which is complementary to other investments.

High entry costs

Despite economic reforms undertaken since the 1980s, entry costs are still relatively high in Africa.[21] Survey data by the World Bank (2007a)[22] show that in 2006, starting a business cost an average of 163 per cent of gross national income (GNI) per capita in sub-Saharan Africa, the highest of all regions (see table 2). Investing in Africa requires an average of 11 procedures, compared with only six in OECD countries.[23] In terms of the time needed to open a business, Latin America and Caribbean countries have the longest waiting period (73 business days), followed by sub-Saharan Africa with 62 days. The shortest waiting period is in OECD countries, where on average only 17 days are required. These regional averages hide important country variations. The cost of entry is lowest in South Africa, where it represents 6 per cent of per capita GNI, followed by Mauritius with 8 per cent and the Seychelles with 9 per cent.[24] At the other extreme are countries such as Sierra Leone, where the cost represents 1,194 per cent of GNI per capita; the Democratic Republic of Congo, where it is 481 per cent; and Niger, with a cost of 416 per cent.

High entry costs are deterrents to investment. In Africa, they are associated with a small formal private sector and a large public sector, measured in terms of formal employment. Before the introduction of SAPs in the 1980s, modern sector employment was concentrated in the public sector in many African countries. In Guinea, for example, state-owned enterprises alone accounted for 76 per cent of formal employment in 1984. The corresponding proportion was 44 per cent in Ghana in 1991, 43 per cent in Zambia in 1980, and 36 per cent in Burundi in 1988 (World Bank, 2005a). However, as SAPs forced African countries to trim their bureaucracies, the resulting "redundant labour" was unable to enter into the formal private sector, partly due to the difficulties associated with entry discussed above. Instead, many of those affected were forced to enter into the informal economy to earn a living. Hence, retrenchment in the public sector had the effect of increasing the "informalization" of economic activities.

Kenya offers a good illustration of how this unfolded in the 1980s and 1990s. The need to reduce budget deficits led to a decline in public sector employment from 30 per cent of total employment in 1990 to 11 per cent in 2000. This "redundant labour" did not migrate to the modern private sector, since the latter also shrank from 36.5 per cent of total employment to 17 per cent over the same period. However, as the formal economy was losing ground, the informal sector thrived. Employment in the non-agricultural informal sector tripled, from about 23 per cent of total employment in 1990 to 70 per cent in 2000 (UNECA, 2005c).

While there are legitimate reasons for controlling entry, for example, in situations where uncontrolled entry could harm consumers' welfare, it is important to recognize that unduly high entry costs as experienced in Africa limit investments and hence their expected welfare effects. Therefore, controls need to be balanced with the need to increase productive investment. Although entry costs are currently high, they can be reduced substantially in a short period. For example, Equatorial Guinea slashed its cost of entry from 2,051 per cent of GNI per capita to 101 per cent in one year between 2005 and 2006. In Ethiopia, the waiting period to start a business was reduced by almost two thirds, from 44 to 16 days between 2003 and 2006 (World Bank, 2007c). This remarkable progress was possible because the respective Governments were willing to reduce these entry costs through a simplification of administrative procedures.

Labour market constraints

There is no consensus among economists on the net benefits of labour regulations. Proponents are of the view that these are essential to ensuring the safety, basic rights and fair compensation of workers. On the other hand, advocates of a flexible labour market argue that these regulations increase the cost of labour, which discourages job creation. Hence, they contend, employment policies must be flexible enough to allow firms to adjust their activities to economic shocks (UNECA, 2005c). Both views are founded. The right balance between protection and flexibility delivers maximum benefits to an economy. A "rigidity of employment index (REI)" is used to empirically assess the situation in Africa (World Bank, 2007c).[25]

Sub-Saharan Africa has an REI of 47 out of 100. In comparison, the REI for OECD countries is 33 and that of the East Asia and Pacific region is 23. There are wide variations across countries. The REI is as low as 7 in Uganda and as high as 78 in the Democratic Republic of the Congo. However, the REI gives only a partial picture of the cost of employment regulations. Non-wage labour costs, which include social security payments and firing costs, are other important components of labour regulations. Sub-Saharan Africa's non-wage labour costs represent about 13 per cent of salary, the third lowest of all regions (see table 2).

Southern African countries, with the exception of Zambia, have very low costs, representing less than 5 per cent of salary. On the other hand, francophone West African countries have among the highest non-wage labour costs, representing 29 per cent of salary in Benin and Congo.[26]

Firing costs, expressed as the number of weeks of wages, represent the cost of advance notice requirements, severance payments and penalties due when terminating a worker. They are highest in sub-Saharan Africa and South Asia, where they represent 71 weeks of wages, compared with 26 weeks in Europe and Central Asia, where they are lowest. Firing costs range from nine to 13 weeks of wages in Gambia and Uganda, respectively, to a staggering 446 and

329 weeks of wages in Zimbabwe and Sierra Leone, respectively. While it is reasonable that workers should be protected against abusive dismissal, requiring a firm to pay almost nine years of salary in case it dismisses a worker, as is the case in Zimbabwe, deters potential employers from hiring workers in the first place.

What lessons may be drawn from the statistics above? Although Africa appears to have put in place costly labour regulations, they have a small average effect on employment and workers' protection, but a large marginal effect on job creation (UNECA, 2005c). The average effect is small because these regulations are only limited to the formal sector, which accounts for a tiny share of the labour force. For example, in the countries forming the Communauté Financière d'Afrique, only about 5 per cent of the labour force is effectively covered by labour regulations, which seem inflexible. However, even when the regulations are in place, they often are not enforced, but this may not be known before entry by potential investors. As a result, few workers are effectively protected by labour regulations. Furthermore, some of these regulations are not binding. For example, minimum wages are set at levels below actual starting wages in many countries, such as in Ghana's and Kenya's manufacturing sector. The disconnect between written regulations and their implementation may explain why empirical studies do not find a statistically significant relationship between hiring and firing rules and the level of unemployment in developing countries.

The fact that the average effect of these regulations on labour markets is small does not mean that they are not important. Whether or not they are enforced, regulations have a strong signalling effect. A potential entrepreneur might decide not to invest if he perceives these regulations as signalling an unfavourable investment environment. Foreign investors, particularly, are most sensitive to the signalling effect of labour regulations for two main reasons. Firstly, they are less able to know that the regulations are not enforced in the domestic economies. Secondly, foreign capital is more mobile, implying that a small difference in labour costs may have a large impact on the location of foreign investment. In this light, the perception of rigidity of African labour markets may help explain why the low level of foreign investment flowing to Africa targets mostly strategic sectors such as extractive industries, with little impact on employment creation (UNECA, 2005c).

The decision facing domestic investors is whether to invest in the formal or informal sector. If they perceive labour regulations in the formal sector to be excessively cumbersome and costly, they might decide to invest in the informal sector. For example, a recent study on India found that States that amended labour regulations in favour of workers experienced a decline in output, employment, investment and productivity in formal manufacturing firms, while output increased in informal manufacturing firms (Besley and Burgess, 2004). Therefore, as for entry costs, labour market regulations should balance the need for workers' protection against the need for investment. After all, it is only by allowing investment to take place that jobs can be created and workers can enjoy their work-related benefits.

Low labour productivity is another important deterrent of investment in Africa, particularly FDI. It has been established that African firms are generally less productive than their counterparts in other developing and developed economies (see Bigsten and Soderbom, 2005). The consequence is that firms try to minimize the amount of labour they hire, even if there is high unemployment and wage rates are low. This prevents the growth of a dynamic labour-intensive manufacturing sector, as has occurred in East Asia. Even countries that have offered foreign investors generous incentives, such as access to export promotion zones, have failed to attract much labour-intensive investment.

Low investor protection

Investor protection can be understood in two different but complementary ways. The first refers to: (a) the extent of disclosure to ensure transparency of transactions; (b) the extent of liability of a firm manager for self-dealing; and (c) the ability of shareholders to sue a company's officers and managers for misconduct (see World Bank, 2007c).[27] Based on these elements, there are no important differences in investor protection between SSA and other regions (see table 2). On a scale of zero to 10, where higher values represent higher protection, the index of investment protection in South Africa and Mauritius is 8 each, the highest in Africa. At the other extreme are Djibouti and Swaziland, each with a score of 2. Botswana, a country hailed for its economic success, has a score of 4, which is below the African average of 4.7 per cent.

One of the most relevant aspects of investor protection in Africa is the vulnerability of firms to arbitrary decisions by public officials, irrespective of the prevailing formal laws and regulations, which can be very costly. For example, Gauthier and Gersovitz (1997) found that medium-sized firms in Cameroon are penalized, as they appear to be the only ones paying taxes. The reason is that small firms in the informal sector could easily evade taxation, if necessary, by shutting down and opening up elsewhere. On the other hand, large firms have enough resources to lobby government officials for tax exemptions. The consequence is that formal investment tends to be confined to large firms, while small firms operate in the informal sector. This could help explain the so-called "missing middle" phenomenon characterizing many developing economies' industrial organization.

Investor protection may also be understood in terms of contract enforcement, the most relevant form of protection in Africa. In the case of a payment dispute over a claim amounting to 200 per cent of GNI per capita in sub-Saharan Africa, it takes on average 581 business days and 38 procedures to settle the case, at a cost representing 42 per cent of the debt. Comparing figures in the rest of the world, South Asia has the longest waiting period, 969 business days, but the number of procedures is similar to that in Africa, and the cost is lower, at 37 per cent of the debt. In Africa, Uganda has the most simplified system, with 19 procedures. The shortest waiting time in Africa is in Gambia, with 247 business days. The cost of settling a dispute is lowest in Algeria and Gabon, where it amounts to 10 per cent of the debt.

The main message is that Africa has among the lowest levels of investment protection. In countries such as the Democratic Republic of the Congo, Malawi, Mozambique and Sierra Leone, settling a business dispute could cost up to twice the amount of the debt. As a result, businesses do not rely on the formal legal system to enforce their commercial contracts. Most prefer to settle their disputes amicably (Fafchamps, 1996).[28] One problem with informal contract enforcement mechanisms is they are unpredictable.

High taxes and a cumbersome tax system

High taxes are often blamed for the low level of investment in African economies. A typical firm in sub-Saharan Africa pays the equivalent of 71 per cent of its profits in taxes, which is 15 percent higher than the second-highest rate, paid in Europe and Central Asia.[29] In countries such as Burundi, the Central African Republic, the Democratic Republic of the Congo, Gambia, Mauritania and Sierra Leone, the amounts of taxes paid by firms are much higher than their net profits. The justification that such poor countries must collect maximum revenue with high tax rates to fund public services and reduce fiscal deficits is challenged by a recent study by McLiesh and Ramalho (2006), which shows that high tax rates lead to low revenue, as they drive firms into the informal sector, reducing the tax base. The study also shows that in poor countries, if the average tax rate paid by businesses is 10 per cent, it would yield revenue equivalent to 16 per cent of GDP; if the tax is increased to 90 per cent, it would yield only about 12 per cent of GDP in tax revenue (McLiesh and Ramalho, 2006: figure 2.1).

Tax payment also has a high bureaucratic cost, understood here as the number of payments required each year. Fifty payments are required in Europe and Central Asia, the highest of all regions, in comparison to 41 payments in sub-Saharan Africa, where making these payments takes 336 hours. These costs are high relative to OECD countries, where 15 payments take 203 working hours. Seychelles has the best record, with firms there making 15 payments in only 76 hours. In some countries, firms are required to spend so much time dealing with tax payments that it becomes preferable to evade taxation.

There are two main messages arising from this information. Firstly, high tax rates and costly tax procedures may discourage investors from investing in Africa's formal sector. Secondly, this tax system encourages tax evasion and capital flight, reducing even further the financial resources available for development. This does not imply, however, that African countries should engage in a "race to the bottom" by competing to attract foreign investors through unreasonably high tax cuts and tax breaks, as observed in many cases of FDI in natural resource projects.[30] In fact, given the importance of tax revenue for public investment, the amount of expected tax from a foreign investment should be one of the key determinants of its economic benefit to the country. Hence, as in the case for entry costs and labour regulations, what countries need to put in place is a simplified and predictable tax system that balances the profit-making interests of investors and revenue generation for the host country.

E. Effect of business environment on gross domestic capital formation

As expected, the difficult business environment in Africa appears to have negatively affected investment. The correlation between a country's rank in terms of its ease of doing business and the rate of fixed capital formation in 2005 was −0.33, which is statistically significant. This negative relationship is illustrated in figure 5.[31]

The focus on domestic economic factors in analyzing this negative relationship stems from the recognition that they are important, but this in no way suggests that external factors are less important. In fact, as chapter 3 argues, Africa's low savings and investment rates are due to a number of economic and non-economic factors, both internal and external. Nevertheless, the focus on domestic factors is due to the fact that, while it is difficult to alter external factors in favour of Africa, it is relatively less costly to improve the domestic environment. There are several administrative measures, some of them discussed in chapter 3, which could substantially improve domestic savings and their efficient investment. For example, creating an environment where formal and microfinance institutions work in symbiosis has the potential to increase savings and improve credit allocation. Moreover, increasing the efficiency of tax collection trough some basic training and better monitoring of tax collectors could double the tax revenue collected by the Goverhment. Reducing tax exemptions could have an additional positive effect on tax revenue.

Figure 5
Capital formation vs. business environment

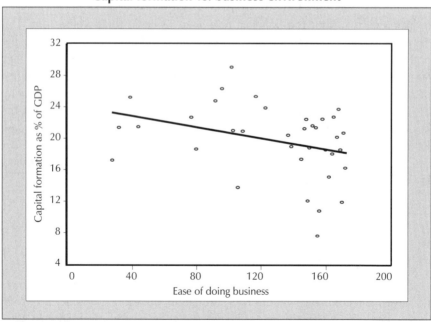

Source: Based on data from World Bank, 2007a and World Bank, 2007c.

Note: Higher ranks on "Ease of doing business" represent poorer business environment.

With respect to the investment climate, it is encouraging that most of the barriers discussed in the chapter can be reduced relatively easily. Indeed, the examples of Equatorial Guinea and Ethiopia have shown how the cost of entry was reduced drastically in a short period. Sudan also reduced its total tax rate from 54 per cent to 37 per cent of profit between 2005 and 2006. Many easy steps can be taken to improve Africa's business environment. For example, unnecessary regulations that increase business costs or send negative signals to investors without serving any purpose should be abandoned. This is the case with some entry requirements and some labour regulations. Indeed, there is ample room for simplifying business regulations simply through the promulgation of appropriate administrative measures.

However, despite the negative correlation between the business environment and capital formation, it would be naïve to expect that reducing the barriers to investment discussed above would lead by itself to an investment boom in Africa. A favourable business environment is not sufficient for achieving increased investment rates. This suggests that, no matter how important these barriers to investment discussed above are, there are other factors, particularly external and political factors, which must be addressed in order to find long-lasting solutions to Africa's low level of savings and investment. Also important to Africa's overall trade and development performance are the global economic environment and multilateral trade rules.

What emerges from the analysis is that action to change the situation in Africa has to come from national Governments, although Africa's development partners also have a role to play to ensure that the global trading environment is not too inimical to Africa's development interests. This notwithstanding, most of the issues discussed above require the State to take the initiative to introduce the measures needed for mobilizing more resources and investing them more efficiently. For example, only the Government can make decisions on the simplification of business procedures. Moreover, some of the problems identified are due to market failures that can only be addressed by government intervention. This is the case, for example, with the provision of law and order, efficient mechanisms for contract enforcement, and basic infrastructure such as roads and electricity, etc., which constitute an essential basis for private investment. In other words, the Government must assume the responsibilities of a developmental State to help Africa emerge from its economic stagnation. Chapter 3 discusses in more detail the argument in favour of developmental States in Africa.

Institutional reform will necessarily form part of any successful development strategy in African countries. It is important, however, to emphasize that there is no set blueprint for an institutional design that promotes development. Indeed, both high-income countries and fast-developing countries have achieved their highest growth rates within an institutional context that was markedly different from that currently advocated by Bretton Woods Institutions and other donors (UNCTAD, 2002). In fact, it has even been suggested that the imposition of institutions that reflect current "best practice" in developed countries, rather than those that have promoted their growth, represents a case of rich countries "kicking away the ladder" with which they themselves climbed to success (Chang, 2002).

Chapter 3

TOWARDS A "DEVELOPMENTAL STATE"

A. Introduction

Despite the ritual implementation of SAPs over the past quarter century, many African countries have yet to experience sustained and robust growth rates high enough to ensure the attainment of the MDGs by the target date. The collapse in both savings and investment continued unabated, until recently. A breakdown in physical infrastructure, combined with a weakening of state capacity to carry out basic public management functions through SAP-induced retrenchment and de-industrialization, increased the size of the informal economy. The continuing lack of diversification of many sub-Saharan African economies also meant that the region's vulnerability to adverse external factors such as commodity price fluctuations did not diminish, and in several cases has rather increased, within the context of trade liberalization.

Since the mid-1990s, several countries have experienced moderate but sustained growth in output. But this growth has been episodic, and in many cases driven by favourable weather (good rainfall) and external environment (mainly high commodity prices), as well as debt relief (within the framework of the Heavily Indebted Poor Countries Initiative) and, since 2000, increased volumes of aid. Considering that macroeconomic stability is the most notable achievement of SAPs, questions are now being asked how the continent could capitalize on this, and also on the newfound mood for democratic dispensation, in order to consolidate economic growth as a means of embarking on a path of sustainable development.

This chapter attempts to map out the common elements of developmental States and examines their applicability (or non-applicability) to Africa. It argues that the necessary ingredients are in place for African countries to tackle their development challenges within the framework of a "developmental State". Increased domestic resources complemented by augmented aid flows are unlikely to provide an escape route from Africa's underdevelopment without a fundamental shift in policy orientation away from the neoliberal stalemate. This is perhaps the only means by which Africa could break into manufacturing export, a strategy developed by almost all benchmark countries (see, for example, Johnson et al., 2007).

B. The developmental State: concept and characteristics

Origins of the concept

The extraordinary economic performance of a group of developing economies in East Asia since the 1960s, which came to be labelled as the first- and second-tier newly industrializing economies (NIEs),[32] has attracted competing explanations. The conventional view attributes the rapid economic development of these economies to trade liberalization and associated export promotion. It contends that the rapid growth of these economies was triggered by market-led outward-oriented development strategies that ensured optimal allocation of resources (see, among others, Fei and Ranis, 1975; Myint, 1982).

In a comprehensive study of these economies, the World Bank was more cautious in its conclusions, to the point of fudging the issues at stake. It identified "market-friendly" policies as part of the policy menu of these countries. At the same time, the Bank acknowledged the role of government policies in the areas of skills acquisition, technological progress, and financial and labour markets (World Bank, 1993). Not surprisingly, therefore, the Bank has been accused of falling prey to the traditional dichotomies of "States versus markets" and "export-oriented versus import substitution", an attitude which is symptomatic of the reluctance or the unwillingness of conventional economists to acknowledge the contributions of heterodoxy to the development debate (Akyüz et al., 1998).

To the non-conventional (heterodox) school, the performance of these countries is underscored by strategic development and industrial policies that derive from a symbiotic relationship between the political and bureaucratic elite and entrepreneurs. A variety of interventionist measures was used to direct resources away from old to new industries in order to alter their long-term development trajectory. The government–business relations that were critical to the success of this strategy were mediated through various institutions and policies. This ensured that subsequent "economic rents" were marshaled to address the objective of rapid economic growth. The institutional and policy framework of these countries also supported their strategic and systematic integration into the global economy (Amsden, 1989, 1991; Wade, 1990; UNCTAD, 1996a, 1997; Akyüz et al., 1998).

The concept of "developmental States" emanated from this last insight into the performance of NIEs, and as such has become associated with the history of development in East Asia. It incorporates a simultaneous and specific combination of economic, political and institutional structures, which have been used heuristically to elucidate the phenomenal economic growth in the NIEs (Sindzingre, 2004). Nevertheless, not all observers who subscribe to this account have the same perspective on the political and economic philosophy, let alone the role of institutions, that underpin the "economic miracle" of the NIEs. Whilst there is some consensus that the NIEs commonly share some characteristics, some analysts are quick to point out that there are important differences between the institutional and policy framework of the first- and second-tier NIEs, as well as among individual countries (see, for example, UNCTAD, 1996a, 1997; Akyüz et al., 1998; Culpepper, 2006).

Various attempts to explain the 1998–1999 Asian financial crisis have also exacerbated the competition among the different explanatory claims. The crisis exposed some of the weaknesses of these economies and triggered a reassessment of the policies, as well as of the concept of the "developmental State" itself. Does "developmental State" contain the seeds (corruption, cronyism, directed credit, fragile financial systems, including weak prudential regulations) of its own destruction, as suggested by the "counter–literature" of neoliberals? (See, for example, Suehiro, 2001.) Have the NIEs simply fallen victim to the ineluctable and destructive forces of globalization and the greed of speculators? Or, as argued by some observers (see, for example, UNCTAD, 1998a, 2000b), did the NIEs simply lose the "Midas touch" and not display the same cautious approach to capital account opening as they did to trade liberalization? Irrespective of our responses to these questions, the fact is that these countries have some useful lessons (positive or otherwise) for other poor developing countries, especially those in sub-Saharan Africa.

Characteristics

The literature distinguishes the developmental State from "non-developmental States" by both its ideology and structure. The ideology of the developmental State is fundamentally "developmentalist", as its major preoccupation is to ensure sustained economic growth and development on the back of high rates of accumulation, industrialization and structural change. Structurally, such a State has (or develops) the capacity to implement economic policies that effectively deliver development, which in turn gives it legitimacy. This capacity is derived from a combination of institutional, technical, administrative and political factors. It is a "strong State" that enjoys autonomy from social forces that might otherwise dissuade it from the use of its capacity to design and implement polices that are in its long-term interest. At the same time, it develops some "social anchoring" that prevents it from the use of its autonomy in a predatory manner, which is what secures it the approval of key social actors (see Castells, 1992; and Myrdal, 1968 in Mkandawire, 2001: 290). Thus, what makes the developmental State effective is not just autonomy, but "embedded autonomy", in which the State is immersed in a network of ties that bind it to groups or classes that can become allies in the pursuit of societal goals (Evans, 1995).

Mkandawire contends, however, that this definition of a developmental State is misleading, as it equates "success" to the strength of the State, whilst measuring this strength by the presumed outcome of its policies. It also emphasizes success at the expense of the "trial and error" nature of policymaking, which is an important feature of even the most successful developmental States. Indeed, in a developmental State, there must be some room for poor performance stemming from "exogenous factors, miscalculation or plain bad luck", as indeed was the case with African developmental States from about the mid-1970s. Therefore, a developmental State is "…one whose ideological underpinnings are developmental and one that seriously attempts to deploy its administrative and political resources to the task of economic development" (emphasis in the original) (Mkandawire, 2001: 291). The ideological underpinnings of state policies are crucial, as these provide the rationale for some of the policies, give legitimacy to some of the sacrifices that might otherwise not be welcome, and bind the ruling class together (Mkandawire, 2001).

UNCTAD's research on the East Asian NIEs[33] reveals that, although there were noticeable differences in these economies, common features could also be identified. The policy and institutional reforms were all implemented simultaneously. However, there are considerable differences between the first- and second-tier NIEs. In particular, the policies of the latter group resulted in competitive resource-based and labour-intensive industries. Most importantly, this research underscores three characteristics which are crucial to the success of the NIEs and therefore critical in the analysis of developmental States. Firstly, institutional reforms and policy interventions revolve around a "profit–

investment nexus", an accumulation dynamic, which is critical to the growth process. Secondly, there are close and interdependent linkages with exports – an "export–investment nexus". Finally, the process of managing "economic rents" ensures their beneficial impact on the development process. In their analysis, Akyüz et al. (1998) suggest that these three principles are more common in the development strategies of the first-tier NIEs (that is, including Japan but excluding Hong Kong, China; see box 1 for a detailed discussion of these principles).

Cleary, this analysis of the development experience of the NIEs (see box 1), indicates that neither the "market" nor the "State" can by itself deliver the ultimate goal of development. The real path to sustainable growth and development emanates from a pragmatic mix of markets and state action, taking into consideration the country-specific development challenges. The experiences of the NIEs, nevertheless, point to some common characteristics of developmental States.[34] Active development strategies, in particular industrial policies, are at the heart of the success of these States in "creating winners" rather than "picking winners". Clear policies and goals are set for the economy in terms of export promotion, investment in human capital and credit allocation via state development banks. Issues of economic coordination were addressed through innovative measures, whilst efforts were directed at minimizing bureaucratic failure (Amsden, 2001). Industrialization was driven by learning processes, borrowing of technology and an array of policies, including targeted taxation, protection, restrictions on foreigner shareholding, financial sector policies that revolve around directed lending, a skilled and educated labour force, including training in the civil service and in technology at tertiary levels, and the development of infrastructure. This is what accounts for differences between Asia and Africa in terms of gross domestic expenditure in research and development and the intensity of that research and development (the ratio of gross domestic expenditure in research and development as a ratio of GDP), which persist today (see table 4). All of these are underscored by long-term relations between political powers and the private sector, and between the banks and public and private firms – the so-called "alliance capitalism". Typically, heterodox economic policies, such as state intervention (targeted on growth) and political rent-seeking, were subjected to market discipline.

Flexibility was built into long-term industrial strategies, whilst short-term, rigid, regulatory measures promoted the strengthening of institutions. Technocratic autonomy was given primacy over political power, although it was embedded in society, as well as in private sector and industrial networks. The strengthening of

Box 1

Newly industrializing economies: dynamics of capital accumulation, export–investment nexus and rent management

The role of capital accumulation in the process of growth and development is reflected in the emphasis on the "profit–investment nexus" in the development strategies of the NIEs. This explains the phenomenal rise in savings and investments in these economies from very low levels in the 1950s. The ratio of gross national savings to GDP, for example, increased dramatically, from around 3 per cent (1951–60) to almost 35 per cent in the early 1990s in the Republic of Korea; from about 10 per cent to 27 per cent in Taiwan Province of China; and from 9 per cent to 34 per cent in Hong Kong, China over the same period. There were also corresponding increases in the ratio of gross domestic investment to GDP over the same period: 10 per cent to 37 per cent in the Republic of Korea; 16 per cent to 23 per cent in Taiwan Province of China; and 9 per cent to 28 per cent in Hong Kong, China (see table 3).

By maintaining political stability, these Governments created a "pro-investment" macroeconomic environment with occasional tolerance towards some degree of inflationary pressure in order to boost investor confidence. When restrictive measures became necessary as a means of balancing national economic development goals, consumption, rather than investment, was first sacrificed. Strong incentives were introduced to boost profits above free-market levels through a variety of fiscal instruments,[a] whilst trade, financial and competition policies[b] were used to create "rents" that boosted corporate profits and therefore the potential investible resources available to corporations. These measures encouraged corporate savings, which in turn boosted capital accumulation. A combination of these incentives (and disciplinary measures)[c] created and sustained a dynamic profit–investment nexus: high profits increased not only the incentives of firms to invest, but also their capacity to finance new investments, and higher investment raised profits by enhancing rates of capital utilization and the rate of productivity growth.

An integral part of East Asian development strategy was policy measures that link the profit–investment nexus to the "export–investment nexus". This is in recognition of the fact that developing countries need not only master off-the-shelf technologies, they must also enhance their competitiveness in mature product markets with established firms.[d] In effect, it is not just the volume or level of investments that is important; the sectors in which these investment are made are equally if not more important.

Investment promotion measures were implemented as an integral part of measures to establish domestic capital and intermediate goods industry and technological upgrading. They were also implemented with other policies, such as a re-institution of import controls, rolling back tax exemptions on the import of some intermediate and capital goods, and granting higher investment tax credits to businesses buying domestically produced machinery. These were combined with polices that enhance technological capacity at the national, industry and firm levels, and tax and other incentives for enterprise training, which were implemented as an integral part of national training programmes. These programmes emphasized technical subjects at higher levels of education and the involvement of industry in vocational training schemes, alongside measures to facilitate local research and development, including direct financial subsidies. A critical link in the process of industrial upgrading was the transfer and adaptation of foreign technology (see table 4).

Box 1 (contd.)

The integration of these economies into the global economy was gradual, strategic and tailored to meeting specific sectoral requirements, which were sequenced in accordance with the level of industrial and economic development. Similarly, the principle of strategic integration was applied to technology transfer. In those sectors in which FDI played a big role (such as textiles and electronics, for example, in Japan, the Republic of Korea and Taiwan Province of China), government policy was vital in promoting joint ventures, screening imported technologies and bargaining over local content requirements. Direct government support was crucial to the process of integrating transnational corporations in a national industrialization strategy.

Of all the unorthodox policies in the development arsenal of the East Asian economies, creating and managing economic rents was probably the most contentious and risky. This is because rents, if not managed properly, could become permanent and not only weaken entrepreneurship but also smother productivity growth in the long run. In the light of these dangers, it was ensured that policies and institutions that created the initial rents to kick-start a development process were eventually withdrawn. Recipients of rents were expected to conform to international market-based disciplines, as they had to meet a combination of performance criteria such as export targets.

A variety of factors was crucial to the successful management of economic rents and in boosting domestic savings, investment and exports (see table 3). Firstly, a strategic alliance with common developmental goals was forged between Government and business institutions, and pivoted on an efficient and meritocratic civil service. Secondly, the evolution and organization of a domestic entrepreneurial class in the form of large diversified corporate groups and conglomerates (as in Japan and the Republic of Korea) and large state-owned enterprises (as in Taiwan Province of China), were important in ensuring the successful outcome of these policies. Thirdly, the process of industrial development spawned a series of formal and informal links with the entrepreneurial class that facilitated the implementation and coordination of policy measures. Finally, institutional links between corporations and banks contributed to the establishment of an improved investment regime. One expression of this was the socialization of risks through state–owned, bank–based lending and state direction of the financial sector as a means of addressing financial sector imperfections.

Source: Akyüz et al., 1998. See also UNCTAD 1996 and 1997.

a   Tax exemptions and special depreciation allowances were applied across the board, but also targeted specific industries as a means of supplementing corporate profits and encouraging profit retention as a means to accelerating capital accumulation.

b   These included a range of selective protection policies, interest rate controls and credit allocation, managed competition (including the encouragement of mergers), coordination of capacity expansion, restrictions on entry into specific industries, and the screening of technology acquisition, among others.

c   A variety of measures was deployed to discourage luxury consumption by potential investors as well as to eliminate speculative investments based on arbitrage, for example, and to restrict the outflow of capital during the initial stages of development.

d   As developing countries operate within their production possibility curve, supporting industrial development requires increasing the propensity to invest and promoting movements along existing learning curves.

Table 3

Gross national savings, gross domestic investment and exports in the Asian NIEs and Africa, 1971–2005

(Per cent of GDP)

	Gross national savings					Gross domestic investment					Export of goods and services				
	1951-1960*	1971-1980	1981-1990	1991-2000	2001-2005	1951-1960*	1971-1980	1981-1990	1991-2000	2001-2005	1951-1960*	1971-1980	1981-1990	1991-2000	2001-2005
Hong Kong SAR, China	9.2	30.9	31.8	31.5	31.4	9.1	26.6	27.0	29.0	22.6	..	86.7	110.8	134.6	169.4
Taiwan Province of China	9.8	..	..	..	..	16.3	30.4	22.8	23.9	19.1	9.6	46.3	53.2	46.6	56.2
Indonesia	..	..	26.7	26.1	27.2	9.2a	19.3	29.2	26.2	22.8	13.6a	23.2	24.2	31.6	33.2
Korea, Republic of	3.3	23.7	31.5	35.8	32.1	10.0	29.0	31.0	34.2	29.8	2.0	26.4	33.5	32.1	39.5
Malaysia	23.2b	..	27.9	35.0	34.0	15.3a	24.9	30.9	34.7	22.4	51.4a	47.7	59.7	96.2	117.8
Singapore	-	28.8	41.8	48.9	40.0	11.4a	41.2	41.2	33.8	20.8	-	156.2	292.2	177.3	214.2
Thailand	15.3	22.7	26.6	33.4	30.0	13.5	28.5	30.7	33.5	26.3	18.3	19.8	26.9	46.3	68.0
Africa	..	..	16.2	15.2	17.9	..	22.4	20.4	21.0	20.3	..	27.5	24.1	27.2	34.9
Sub-Saharan Africa	..	**23.5**	**17.5**	**14.4**	**16.4**	..	**21.4c**	**19.5c**	**21.0c**	**20.1c**	..	**26.0**	**23.7**	**28.1**	**35.7**

Source: World Bank, *World Development Indicators*, online, May 2007.

  a 1960 only.

  b Including Singapore, which became independent in 1963, having enjoyed self-government between 1955 and 1963.

  c Gross domestic investment for sub-Saharan Africa (excluding South Africa).

  * Akyüz et al. (1998) from UNCTAD database.

institutions stimulated economic growth, which in turn strengthened democratic traditions and dispensation. While not often mentioned, social policies were an important ingredient in the arsenal of developmental States. These policies revolved around non-state entities such as families and firms, with the State guaranteeing the implementation of social welfare programmes. Finally, all these countries, with the exception of Hong Kong, China, were highly selective in their liberalization and export-oriented strategies, often ensuring the development of a competitive sector before opening it up (UNCTAD, 1996a, 1997; Akyüz et al., 1998; Wade, 2003).

The development process in the developmental States has been described as an institutional interventionist solution (to the problems of underdevelopment) pivoted on the principle of reciprocity. There is a "reciprocal control mechanism", whereby Governments provide assistance (e.g. subsidies) to the manufacturing sector, which then reciprocates by meeting a performance standard (e.g. export target). Governments tried "getting the control mechanisms 'right'", rather than trying to get "prices right" (Amsden, 2001).

It is certainly difficult to be prescriptive in all these policy areas in attempting to identify a "replicable strategy", if that were at all possible, for attaining a fast pace of development for poor developing countries, such as those in sub-Saharan Africa. However, in view of the pivotal role played by the financial sector in rapidly boosting domestic savings and in development strategies in the developmental States of East Asia, the sections below endeavour to identify some broad policy lessons for African countries. Considering that Africa probably faces much more severe constraints in the real sector, which contribute low total factor productivity growth than East Asia previously did, these constraints might have to be addressed first as a condition for efficient and effective use of credit.

C. Financial sector reforms: curbing government intervention to cure "financial repression"

Bringing about a developmental State necessitates (re)defining the roles for some of the State's major institutions, or in some respects, adopting new ways of performing existing tasks. One such institution is the central bank, which was used by both early and new industrializers of all stripes to support their development strategies (see box 2). The need to rethink the role of the financial system or the banking sector in development in poor countries is nothing new. Financial sector reforms featured prominently in broader SAPs implemented by most sub-Saharan African economies beginning in the early 1980s. Financial sector reforms, particularly in the commercial banking sector, were grafted onto the main SAPs from about the late 1980s.

The main objective of these reforms was to address "financial repression", low or negative real interest rates stemming from financial restrictions, mainly government policies that discourage savings and capital accumulation and optimal allocation of resources (McKinnon, 1973; and Shaw, 1973). The reforms therefore aimed at attaining a more effective, robust and deeper financial system via the introduction of market forces, to enable it to support the private sector as an engine of growth in these economies. At the heart of the reforms was the enhancement of the quality of financial services, underscored by positive real interest rates, in order to attain improved savings mobilization and credit allocation. Other objectives were to reduce government intervention in directing

Table 4
Mind the technology gap: East Asia and Africa

A. Technology: diffusion and creation, 1990 and 2004

	Telephone mainlines (per 1,000 people)		Cellular subscribers (per 1,000 people)		Internet users (per 1,000 people)	
	1990	2004	1990	2004	1990	2004
Developing countries	21	122	*	175	*	64
East Asia and Pacific	18	199	*	262	*	91
Latin America and Caribbean	61	179	*	319	0	115
South Asia	7	35	*	42	0	29
Sub-Saharan Africa	**10**	**	*	77	0	19
OECD	390	491	10	714	3	484

Source: UNDP, 2006.

*   Greater than zero but small enough that the number would round to zero at the displayed number of decimal points.

**   Data not available.

B. Gross expenditure on research and development (GERD) and research and development intensity/GDP, 1990 and 1999/2000

	1990		1999/2000	
	GERD (billions)	GERD/ GDP (%)	GERD (billions)	GERD/ GDP (%)
Developed countries	367.9	2.3	596.7	2.3
Developing countries	42.0	0.7	158.4	0.9
Latin America and Caribbean	11.3	0.5	21.3	0.6
Africa	**5.2**	**0.6**	**5.8**	**0.3**
South Africa	2.9	1.0	3.6	0.8
Other SSA countries	1.9	0.5	1.1	0.2
Arab States in Africa (N. Africa)	0.4	0.3	1.1	0.2
Asia	94.2	1.8	235.6	1.5
Japan	67.0	3.1	98.2	2.9
China	12.4	0.8	50.3	1.0
India	2.5	0.8	20.0	0.7
NIEs in Asia	8.2	1.6	48.2	1.7

Source: UNESCO, 2004.

credit or setting interest rates, and to increase competition contingent upon liberalized entry and/or removal of other competition-limiting regulations (see Brownbridge and Gayi, 1999).[35]

These objectives were enunciated in new banking legislation such as new financial sector or banking acts, which also re-emphasized the role of central banks as guarantors of the entire banking system through a strengthening of prudential regulation and supervision of banks. Banking supervision, monitoring and control were to be streamlined and improved by training of existing staff and new recruits to enforce new guidelines on higher minimum capital adequacy requirements, lending policies (e.g. which ban insider lending), regular on-site inspections and early intervention in distressed banks.

While the reforms emphasized the application of market principles in the banking sector, they were ambivalent about the independence of central banks beyond a reduction of the influence of Government on its operations, together with a more stringent enforcement of prudential regulation and supervisory requirements. They had far-reaching implications for commercial bank operations, and more importantly for the operations of "development banks", which were forced to comply with the new banking regulations if they took deposits. This led to the abandonment of the original development objectives of these banks. They were forced into short-term credit and service programmes, in contrast to their original objective of medium- to long-term finance[36] (Garson, 2006).

Overall, the reforms have, to different degrees (and with varying levels of success), made the financial sector of these countries more susceptible to the application of commercial principles in their deposit taking, lending and borrowing operations. The reforms are still ongoing in some countries, but the verdict to date suggests that they have not met their original objectives in several areas. Few innovative financial products have been introduced, oligopoly has frustrated competition, and whatever limited entry there has been into the financial sector is concentrated in the urban areas. In the context of privatization of previously state-owned commercial banks and the subsequent closure of the branches of these banks in rural areas, the new financial sector that has emerged from these reforms tends to induce commercial banks to set up in urban areas (now overserved) rather than in rural areas which are underserved, if served at all (UNCTAD, 1996b; Brownbridge and Gayi, 1999). The reforms also facilitated the entry of specialized financial institutions, including non-bank financial

Box 2
The role of central banks in development

The current conception of central banks is that they should be politically independent from Governments, with a functional focus on fighting inflation by means of indirect monetary policy instruments, such as short-term interest rates, to influence the level of economic activity. As Epstein (2005) points out, however, this notion represents only a partial reading of their history. Central banks of all persuasions (say, the Bank of England, the United States Federal Reserve and even the Bank of France and Bank of Japan) have historically all financed Governments, managed exchange rates, and employed various policy measures to support preferred economic sectors.a This was a mission in which all tools of direct monetary policy were considered legitimate, ranging from subsidized interest rates, legal restrictions and directed credit, to moral suasion to promote particular markets and institutions. The historical accounts of various central banks are replete with instances of their engagement in "industrial policy" or "selective targeting".

While central banking underwent dramatic transformation in the developing world in the aftermath of World War II, in the late 20th century these banks were used as agents of economic development more extensively in some developing countries than in developed ones. This was partly in response to the concern of Governments to be able to pursue monetary policy designed to promote more rapid economic development and to mitigate excess swings in national money incomes. Most central banks in these so-called "late industrializers" (including the NIEs) in the post-war period continued with their developmental role, i.e. with policies designed to develop their economies, such as selective credit controls, the creation of special credit institutions to cater to the needs of specific sectors (agricultural and industrial development banks), and redistribution of real resources between the public and private sectors. [b]

Some of these policies have been criticized in the last three decades or so, but it is not incorrect to say that central bank support for development in the "late industrializers" is a critical part of their development story. The role of finance, in particular mobilization and allocation of medium and long-term finance for industrialization, was pivotal in their development performance. The "development bank" model, sometimes with the whole banking sector "acting as a surrogate development bank", was deployed in particular to finance investments of targeted industries by channelling long-term credit[c] on concessionary terms. By keeping the effective real interest rates low (in some cases even negative), and using capital controls to keep out hot money[d] (and thereby avoiding overvalued exchange rates), central banks facilitated the realization of the specific development objectives of Governments. These policies were not always successful, but were critical in underscoring the level of economic development attained in these countries in a generation.

The current tendency is for neoliberals to argue that the role of central banks should be the stabilization of the economy by means of "inflation targeting". This assertion does not stand up to historical evidence with either the European early industrializers or in the Asian late industrializers. Historically, central banks have been most effective as vehicles of development (more so in the NIEs or the "late industrializers" than in the developed countries) when used to promote the industrial policies of Governments. The vexing issue is what sort of balance they should maintain between their developmental and stabilizing roles. In the context of poor developing countries, it may not be appropriate for central

---

Box 2 (contd.)

banks to redefine this developmental role as the promotion of "stock market-based" financial sectors.[e]

Sources: Brimmer, 1971, Amsden, 2001, and Epstein, 2005.

a   The Bank of France and the Bank of Japan have deployed credit allocation to support industrial policy, whilst the Bank of England and the United States Federal Reserve have promoted the financial sectors of their economies consonant with the international role of their financial services industries (Epstein, 2005).

b   This is particularly the case for China, India, Indonesia, the Republic of Korea, Malaysia, Taiwan Province of China and Thailand in Asia; and for Argentina, Brazil, Chile and Mexico in Latin America (see Amsden, 2001).

c   Public finance for this was "off-budget" – non-tax revenues from foreign sources, deposits in government-owned banks, post office savings accounts and pension funds.

d   These are inflows of speculative capital that flow out immediately at the least sign of any instability in host economies.

e   There is little evidence that these sectors, which have been promoted in recent years in many developing countries, lead to faster growth or indeed more development (Epstein, 2005). To date, the history of stock market development in Africa is not encouraging. Most, if not all, of the 21 stock exchanges on the continent not only have low levels of liquidity and suffer from a lack of integration with regional and global markets, they also suffer from technological and capacity constraints (see UNECA, 2007: 7). And indeed, internal and external financial liberalization (capital account opening) as a means of promoting the development of the financial sector can make developing countries more vulnerable to financial market instability, as was the case in recent financial crises: the East Asian financial crisis of 1997–1998, the financial collapse in Russia in 1998, Brazil in 1999 and in 2002, the Central Asian Republics in 1998–2000, and in Argentina in 1995 and 2001–2002 (see, for example, UNCTAD , 1996, 1997; Griffith-Jones, 1998; Jomo, 2005; Khor, 2005; and Taylor, 2007).

institutions, although the closure of some "development banks" has left some financial service gaps (Garson, 2006). The biggest casualties of these reforms are the "development banks", whose objectives and mission are perceived to be incongruent with the underlying neoliberal rationale of reforms. Some of these banks were admittedly closed because of insolvency (see, for example, UNCTAD, 1996b; Brownbridge and Gayi, 1999). However, it is arguable if an entire policy should have been ditched because of this, or whether an attempt should have been made to restructure their assets, as was done in the case of some commercial banks through non-performing asset recovery trusts.

It cannot be denied that the emerging financial sector does not respond to the financial and developmental needs of African countries. Low levels of savings (held as financial assets) persist, even in those countries that have resumed growth since the mid-1990s. Worryingly, there is excess liquidity in the banking system, which suggests an inability to convert even the low levels of savings mobilized into investments.[37] Whatever increase there has been in domestic investment, as discussed earlier, has been financed mostly by foreign capital, in particular the resurgence in ODA flows, but also debt relief (McKinley, 2005). There is therefore a need to re-engineer financial institutions in a way that addresses the specific developmental issues in African countries, that is, institutions that fill the void for term finance in the formal sector as well as the financing gaps for small and medium-sized enterprises and other firms in the informal sector. This will require complementary changes in monetary policy stances of individual countries. A starting point may be to revisit the role of central banks in order to see how they can function as the leading development agents in these countries (see box 2 for how central banks were used to promote development in Europe, the United States and the Asian NIEs).

What role for the financial sector in development?

Much of Africa's previously non-competitive, shallow and "repressive" financial system could be traced to the implementation of some of these same policies (as in box 2) entailed in the development bank model by Governments (Brownbridge and Gayi, 1999). However, as illustrated in the case of the NIEs, there was nothing intrinsically bad about these policies (see also next section). The external environment, overall macroeconomic context, quality of governance and associated political direction, and mode of implementation are what make a difference to the outcome of the implementation of this set of policies. Clearly, Africa has made significant progress in attaining macroeconomic stability and improving governance across the region, and is serious about tackling in a concerted manner its development challenges (for example, as expressed in the objectives of the New Partnership for Africa's Development (NEPAD)). A new institutional landscape has emerged pivoted on the African Union (including NEPAD),[38] and the Regional Economic Communities. Coupled with this are new Pan-African governance structures such as the Pan-African Parliament, the African Court on Human and Peoples' Rights and the African Peer Review Mechanism (APRM)[39]. More than 40 African countries have also ratified the United Nations Convention Against Corruption and 18 countries have signed up to the Extractive Industries Transparency Initiative. Thus, these policies now stand a much better chance of yielding the desired outcomes within a strengthened macroeconomic, institutional, and more transparent and accountable environment.

However, doubts have emerged recently as to whether African countries could sustain their improved growth performance since the mid-1990s without a clearly defined development strategy. This is because, notwithstanding the recent improvements in economic fundamentals, some problems have persisted in keeping the economies trapped in a low growth trajectory. As discussed in chapters 1 and 2, economic growth has produced only a limited number of jobs in the formal sector, as the extractive sectors leading growth are capital-intensive and have very limited linkages to the rest of the economy. Lending to the private sector has remained limited, averaging about 20 per cent of GDP. Despite financial sector reforms, banks still prefer to lend only to established firms, mostly foreign affiliates, for a variety of reasons.[40] The sale of government debt to finance the budget means that most banks hold their assets in government papers (treasury bills), which carry virtually no risks. The financial sector lacks competition, the result of which is very high interest rates (despite low and falling inflation) and high spreads,[41] which discourage all but the most determined local investors and long-term investments (see also Chapter 2). Banks are also careful to avoid a mismatch between their assets and liabilities; most attract only short-term deposits which could not be used to fund long-term investments in particularly risky environments.

Thus, the outcomes of financial sector reforms in these countries to date are not promising for the emergence of a commercially-oriented banking system that is likely to plug the gap for long-term investment needs. The short supply of term financing will almost certainly continue into the foreseeable future. All these call for a determined government financial sector action or policy in favour of long-term financing and credit provision to the neglected small and medium-sized enterprises and entrepreneurs, for whom access to credit is a problem (see also Chapter 2).

Long-term public debt instruments will not only encourage the financing of public investments in infrastructure, water and energy, but they will also facilitate the management of government debt, just as direct loans to employment intensive sectors (McKinley, 2005) may be an antidote to the region's current jobless growth. Within the current context, this would probably involve a substitution of existing short-term debt with long-term debt in several countries. However, whatever policy is adopted in this specific instance has to be consistent with the overall government monetary policy stance, in particular regarding the level of its fiscal deficits. Also, a clearly-defined policy on long-term financing within the context of an overall development strategy predicated on development banks could provide financing for domestic investors in the Government's strategic sectors (see chapter 4 for a detailed discussion).

In the rural areas, the key to developing financial markets is to find the institutional arrangements which can best overcome the specific types of market failures afflicting these markets.[42] As such, there may also be the need to encourage the growth of different types of non-bank financial institutions to serve those segments of financial markets which are unattractive to the commercial banks. Leasing companies could provide a potentially useful vehicle for short- to medium-term asset financing for small and medium-sized enterprises within an appropriate legal framework, ensuring that they are being subjected to prudential regulation and supervision if they are to mobilize funds from the market (Brownbridge and Gayi, 1999). These could be joint public–private partnerships. Considering the pervasive nature of market failures in rural financial markets, some government intervention to facilitate credit supply to small farmers and rural small and medium-sized enterprises could improve social welfare. If these farmers and entrepreneurs operate in sectors that correspond to priorities, such loans could be subsidized.

Most African economies have attained macroeconomic stability, probably about the only notable achievement of SAPs. Inflation rates declined from double digits during the 1980s to single digits in most countries by the end of the 1990s. By 2004, only three of 52 African countries had inflation rates of more than 20 per cent. In 2006, the inflation rates for 40 of the 52 countries were in single digits, with another 10 posting rates of between 10 and 19.9 per cent (UNECA, 2007: 41). Macroeconomic instability is therefore no longer the main issue for most African countries. And considering the fact that there is a lack of consensus on the threshold at which the negative effects of inflation kick in, Governments would appear to have some leeway in terms of policy. While some studies suggest that this threshold is as low as 10 per cent, others, such as McKinley (2005: 20), indicate that this level could be as high as 20 to 25 per cent.

Despite the outbreak of new civil unrest in a few countries, some of the worst conflicts in the history of the continent have now ended. As discussed earlier, most Governments are now committed to good governance as well as to development within the framework of new pan-African institutional and governance structures. So the chances are that a commitment to enhancing growth, creating employment, and reducing poverty via a loosening of fiscal policy, including directed credit to strategic sectors, is most likely to produce favourable economic outcomes.

The original arguments in favour of liberalizing the financial sector as advanced by McKinnon (1973) and Shaw (1973) still resonate with several economists.[43] On the other hand, some economists support some forms of financial repression, particularly given the economic and political structures, including institutional weaknesses, of many developing countries (and against the background of the experiences of the NIEs).[44] This latter group contends that the removal of one distortion might not necessarily enhance welfare in the presence of other distortions. Similarly, financial liberalization is unlikely to improve welfare much, given the prevalence of information asymmetries afflicting financial transactions and markets (see, for example, Stiglitz, 2000). The recent bouts of financial crises in several emerging economies appear to have vindicated the position of the critics of financial liberalization. Indeed, the poor sequencing of financial sector reforms in Africa[45] suggests that even if the benefits of liberalization were guaranteed, these would depend largely on how reforms were implemented. And the prevalence of financial dualism (as discussed in chapter 1) suggests the need for caution in recommending liberalization policies for countries in the region. This is particularly so because, as observed by Gemech and Struthers (2003), financial dualism has rarely been adequately incorporated in empirical studies on financial liberalization. Nevertheless, some observers have noted that financial liberalization has had a somewhat positive effect on the informal financial sector, and to the extent that fragmentation in financial markets is replaced by segmentation, liberalization could prove useful to these economies (Steel et al., 1997).

In the light of the observations above, it might not be unreasonable that some form of government action to fix the weaknesses of the financial sector in African economies is actually welfare enhancing. This should take the form of flexible monetary policy that aims to create more jobs rather than attaining lower rates of inflation, and the regulation of capital accounts to contain capital flight. Policy measures are also necessary to facilitate the mobilization of domestic resources (e.g. via pension or social security funds) and directing these into long-term, productive, employment- generating investments, e.g. by credit allocation and subsidies (see chapter 4).

These fiscal and monetary policies could be complemented with measures to underpin a profit–investment nexus. This is critical not only to domestic capital accumulation on a self-sustaining basis, but also for channelling capital into strategic sectors that propel the economy onto a higher growth trajectory.

Irrespective of the conclusions on the causative factors of the financial crisis that engulfed the Asian economies in the late 1990s, a major lesson from the crisis is that a strong financial sector is central to the prevention of such a crisis, and to the pace of recovery from it. Prudential regulation of banks and strong banking supervision to ensure the implementation of such regulation are the hallmarks of such a financial system. The capacities of Governments to implement the kinds of policies discussed in this section depend on the quality of institutions, governance and macroeconomic stability.

D. Can Africa nurture "developmental States"?

There have been several attempts to distil lessons from the East Asian experiences for other parts of the developing world, including sub-Saharan Africa (see, for example, UNCTAD, 1996, 1997, 1998; Akyüz et al., 1998; Mkandawire, 2001; and Sindzingre, 2004). In the case of sub-Saharan Africa, several observers have expressed doubts not only about the quality of institutional infrastructure, but also about the capacity of sub-Saharan African States to design, implement and monitor complex and demanding policies such as those that have been at the core of the success of the NIEs. Much of this conclusion is premised on the assumption that African States are too corrupt and predatory, and ruled by rent-seeking or just plain kleptocratic officials who prioritize their private interests over those of the State, and use rents to fund patronage for their constituents.[46]

This view of the African State is prevalent today in the literature and among some African observers and students, but it is distorted. It describes, in a rather sweeping and general sense (and without a critical analysis of their differential performances), the so-called "African State" at a particular historic juncture in the continent's development trajectory – mainly from about the mid-to-late 1970s. In reality, this conception of the "African State" refers, in part, to some States in social and political turmoil, their poor economic performance being just one manifestation of such a State. It is derived from "ideological, paradigmatic and structural shifts in both domestic and international spheres"[47] (Mkandawire, 2001), in particular from the anti-State rhetoric associated with the 1980s' neoliberalism. As such, it is based more on ideological preference rather than a careful analysis of the role and effectiveness of the State (UNCTAD, 2006a).

Africa's economic malaise: domestic policy mistakes?

The extent to which Africa's economic performance could be attributed to the impact of external and internal factors has often been contested. But it appears the role of exogenous factors is often underestimated. This failure to take full account of the exogenous factors as explanatory variables in diagnosing Africa's development malaise has led to a misunderstanding and, as a result, misleading statements concerning Africa's development problem. For example, according to Mkandawire (2001: 303), the World Bank's 1981 Berg Report "...had in many ways misrepresented Africa's economic performance during the preceding two decades ... [It] underestimated the enormous importance to African economies of external conjuncture and the role of foreign expertise".

The World Bank identified "structural" factors (evolving from historical circumstances or from the physical environment) and external factors as impeding Africa's economic growth. Nevertheless, in its view, these were exacerbated by "domestic policy inadequacies", to which the main thrust of its policy recommendations were directed (World Bank, 1981), thus laying the foundation for the neoliberal paradigm which was manifested in structural adjustment policies. This emphasis on the internal factors has been traced to the intellectual debate, in which Africa was caught up, within the World Bank (and the economic profession) during the Robert McNamara era.[48] The increasing popularity of the neoliberals in a way led to an uncritical acceptance of the analysis of the Berg Report by most African observers (Mkandawire, 2001; Arrighi, 2002: 30-32). As such, there appeared to be no opposition (or alternative)[49] to the report's policy prescriptions, which held sway on the continent for the best part of three decades, with catastrophic consequences (see, for example, UNCTAD, 2002; Arrighi, 2002: 32).

Historical imprints: volatile mix of external and internal factors

One might not go as far as Sindzingre to repudiate the role of the State in promoting growth in Asia, but one can characterize particular economic outcomes as stemming "...rather from particular modalities and actualizations of the concept of the State, from specific historical trajectories and combination of institutions and individual expectations" (Sindzingre, 2004). The State in much of Africa is a product of competition between colonial powers for access to resources of the continent with seemingly little, if any, concern for already existing societal arrangements revolving around ethnic conglomerations. This history has left some distinctive imprints on the evolution of States (or post-colonial Governments) in Africa (see also Arrighi, 2002: 24). These States are, as a result, products of certain historical and geopolitical developments which continue to inform the nature of politics, which can be subject to interference and/or manipulation by external powers. But whilst the concept of "State" as in the European context may be foreign to Africa (and "statehood" may be in its infancy, the very basis of the State still being a subject of contention in some countries), there were great expectations of the leaders of the independence struggle not only to end colonial rule but also to deliver as fast as possible on development in the post-colonial African State.

In the immediate post-colonial period of the 1960s and early 1970s, most sub-Saharan African countries had fairly strong Governments that took the task of nation-building and development seriously. Not surprisingly, therefore, they managed to attain and sustain positive and in several cases robust economic growth rates. However, a lethal combination of external shocks (sharp rises in the price oil and collapse in the prices of their major primary commodity exports) triggered economic collapse starting from about the late 1970s. This was the genesis of the African debt crisis of the 1980s and the 1990s. As argued elsewhere by UNCTAD, the commodity-dependent nature of these countries makes them extremely vulnerable not only to declining terms of trade but also to the commodity price variability (UNCTAD, 2003; Sindzingre, 2004).

Within one year, the ratio of exports of good and services to GDP in Africa and sub-Saharan Africa collapsed respectively from 33 and 31 per cent (1974) to 27 and 25 per cent (1975) and never recovered in a sustained manner until 2000. This ratio was much higher in Africa in 1974 (at the time the crisis set in) than in Indonesia (28 per cent), the Republic of Korea (27 per cent) and Thailand (22 per cent). In the ensuing years, all these countries had overtaken Africa, the Republic of Korea since 1981 reaching an export/GDP ratio ranging from 41 to 44 per cent from 2000 to 2005, and Thailand since 1988 reaching an export/GDP ratio of 67 to 74 per cent in 2000–2005, compared with Africa's 33 to 38 per cent over the same period. While Indonesia outperformed Africa from 1997 to 2001, its performance on this indicator since 2002 has more or less been the same as Africa's (see table 3).

In some African countries, the dire economic situation induced political instability, which in turn exacerbated the former during much of the 1980s, thereby increasing the vulnerability of the State to capture by various special interest groups. The complex interplay of economic and political regress, the outcome of the competition between these domestic forces for the control of State power and resources to serve private ends, consigned several of these countries to a category that was later to be christened as "failed" or "weak" States.

The implementation of SAPs from the early 1980s, whilst restoring some macroeconomic stability, did not start a process of strong economic recovery, structural transformation, nor indeed economic diversification. Throughout much of the 1990s, average economic performance throughout the region was anaemic, averaging about 3 per cent per annum with a sustained recovery starting only from about the turn of the century. Economic growth has since averaged 4.6 per cent per annum between 2000 and 2005. In 2006, the continent's average growth rate was 5.7 per cent, and this is projected to increase to about 6.2 per cent in 2007 (UNECA, 2007).

In sum, several analysts have argued that developmental States are unlikely to emerge from this economic, political and social milieu for a variety of reasons.[50] These include the poor record of economic performance until recently, and "softness" of the African State and its vulnerability to capture by special interest groups, as well as its lack of a development ideology. The other reasons are the dependence of the State on external resources, the lack of technical and analytical capacity, and the changed international environment in which protectionist industrial policies have been outlawed (or have to meet more stringent requirements) under the World Trade Organization (WTO) Agreements (Mkandawire, 2001).

Rereading Africa's economic history

Nevertheless, as observed by several scholars (Bangura, 1992; Mkandawire, 2001; and Arrighi, 2002), a more realistic assessment of the political and economic history of the continent reveals a very different picture from this truncated version. A majority of the first generation of African leaders were preoccupied with development as well as nation-building, to the extent that the post-colonial State in Africa has been dubbed "developmentalist" by some observers,[51] despite earlier criticisms.

Africa's economic performance has not always been as dismal as is usually portrayed in the literature, in particular considering its growth record during the period 1960–1975 (see, for example, Bangura, 1992: 60–61; and Mkandawire, 2001). An analysis of the development experience in most developing countries (i.e. those that experienced at least a 3 per cent growth in GDP per capita) over this period reveals that 11 of the best-performing 50 countries are in Africa (and nine in sub-Saharan Africa). The fastest-growing developing country up to 1975 was African (Gabon), and Botswana's growth rate from 1960 to 1975 exceeded that of Hong Kong (China), Taiwan Province of China, Malaysia and Thailand (Rodrik, 1997) (see also table 5).

An examination of the growth performance of developing countries from 1967 to 1980 yielded similar results. Of the 27 countries that attained the annual growth rate of 6 per cent over more than a decade (taken as a measure of successful development experience) during this period, more than a third (10) were African. In addition to mineral-rich countries such as Gabon, Botswana, the Republic of Congo and Nigeria, other countries such as Kenya and Côte d'Ivoire also outperformed Indonesia and Malaysia. Most interestingly, much of this growth was driven by domestic savings, which increased considerably in the immediate post-independence period, reaching an average annual growth of 23.5 per cent of GDP between 1971 and 1980. By 1980, about a third of sub-Saharan African countries had saving/GDP ratios of more than 25 per cent. Both savings and investment rates in the high-performing African countries over this period were close to those of the NIEs in East Asia (see table 3). However, these savings and investment rates yielded lower growth rates in the former (Mkandawire, 2001: 304–305), a fact which could probably be explained by lower average total factor productivity growth[52] in sub-Saharan Africa (0.83 per cent) relative to East Asia and the Pacific (1.18 per cent) between 1960 and 1973. GDP growth per worker was also lower in sub-Saharan Africa (1.80 per cent) than in East Asia and the Pacific (3.83 per cent) (see table 6). In addition to this good economic performance, Africa attained significant progress in social and physical infrastructure development over this period.

Africa's economic collapse: an eclectic thesis?

How then did most African countries come to grief from about the mid-1970s onward? As argued by UNCTAD (2004), the two oil price shocks of 1973–1974 and 1979–1980 were a significant factor in the economic collapse (and the subsequent debt crisis) of African countries, the latter leading to deterioration in the external environment which lasted until 1982. The rise in oil prices had an adverse impact on the trade balance of oil-importing countries, not only

Table 5
Per capita GDP growth rates: top 50 developing countries, 1960–1975
(Percentage)

Country	1960–75	1975–89	Country	1960–75	1975–89
Gabon	7.87	-3.40	Ireland	4.02	2.70
Singapore	7.40	5.10	Finland	3.99	2.73
Japan	7.05	3.53	Thailand	3.94	4.72
Republic of Korea	6.47	7.00	Italy	3.89	2.80
Botswana	6.16	6.17	Turkey	3.85	1.23
Greece	6.15	1.73	Iceland	3.80	2.54
Hong Kong, China	6.12	6.61	Belgium	3.78	2.08
Lesotho	6.00	2.15	Norway	3.76	2.77
Taiwan Prov. of China	5.86	6.57	France	3.73	1.90
Portugal	5.68	2.59	Austria	3.71	2.29
Spain	5.66	1.64	Dominican Republic	3.56	1.14
Syrian Arab Republic	5.61	0.30	Canada	3.52	2.57
Malta	5.46	5.39	Togo	3.49	0.22
Yugoslavia*	5.42	1.04	Netherlands	3.48	1.35
Israel	4.98	1.25	South Africa	3.39	-0.39
Swaziland	4.76	-0.86	Mexico	3.37	0.76
Barbados	4.60	2.57	Utd. Rep. of Tanzania	3.37	n.a.
Islamic Rep. of Iran	4.59	-3.60	Côte d'Ivoire	3.30	-1.56
Brazil	4.57	1.27	Jamaica	3.23	-1.35
Morocco	4.27	2.20	Bolivia	3.19	-0.77
Malaysia	4.26	3.82	Nicaragua	3.11	n.a.
Nigeria	4.15	-2.41	Costa Rica	3.05	0.82
Tunisia	4.14	2.25	Sweden	3.05	1.45
Panama	4.13	-0.38	Egypt	3.04	2.93
Ecuador	4.04	0.48	Papua New Guinea	3.02	-1.27

Source: Pen World Tables in Rodrik, 1997.
 * Encompassing all current and former Yugoslavian countries.

undermining domestic investment, but also triggering fiscal crises in most of these countries. The second shock coincided with sharp rises in real interest rates and the global recession of 1981–1982, which depressed demand for African exports. The terms of trade deteriorated, and the balance-of-payments crisis afflicting developing countries was exacerbated for oil importers. However, based on the erroneous assumption that quick recovery from the global recession would soon restore the prices of non-fuel commodities, most of these countries resorted to external borrowing to finance fiscal and external imbalances.[53]

For many African countries, there was little room for manoeuvre because of their non-diversified economies, but mostly because of the steep decline in non-fuel primary commodity prices during the global recession of 1981–82.[54] The developmental States of Asia and sub-Saharan Africa have a common feature of external orientation; that is, dependence on external trade to drive their economies. The difference between the two groups was that the Asian economies were more diversified in terms of the technological intensity and composition of exports, whilst their sub-Saharan African counterparts relied almost exclusively on unprocessed primary commodity exports. Paradoxically, therefore, the failure to pursue a labour-intensive "export–oriented strategy" cannot explain the economic collapse of sub-Saharan African countries in the wake of adverse external factors from about the mid-to-late 1970s. These countries, if anything, followed the textbook advice of exploiting their comparative advantage in land-intensive exports (mineral and primary commodities).

Indeed, if there was any "failure" in development policy formulation, it was the lack of a strategy for countries to diversify their economic bases through, for example, an explicit export–investment nexus (Mkandawire, 2001; Arrighi, 2002). As illustrated by the example of the Asian NIEs, progress in increasing the technology intensity of exports is a means of addressing vulnerability and dependence, and remaining on a sustainable growth trajectory (Sindzingre, 2004). Some studies also suggest much of the variance in growth performance during the adjustment period in Africa could be due to differences in productivity and export performance in the industrial sector (Pieper, 2000; Thirlwall, 2004).

The external environment (specifically, the geopolitical context) of sub-Saharan Africa and the NIEs was also markedly different. By virtue of their different geographical locations, the antagonists of the Cold War had different relations with each of these groups, which produced diverse outcomes. Preferential access provided by the United States to its domestic market for its Asian allies was critical in the "take-off" of the region, as were the large amounts of aid it provided. The Korean War, for example, has been described as "Japan's Marshall Plan": over the period 1950–1970, United States aid to Japan averaged $500 million per year. Huge amounts of military and economic aid to the Republic of

Table 6

Economic performance by period and region

(Annual average growth rates, in per cent)

	1960–1974			1975–1984			1985–2000			1960–2000		
	Contribution of growth in education per worker	GDP per worker	TFP*	Contribution of growth in education per worker	GDP per worker	TFP*	Contribution of growth in education per worker	GDP per worker	TFP*	Contribution of growth in education per worker	GDP per worker	TFP*
Sub-Saharan Africa	0.18	1.80	0.83	0.27	-0.76	-1.48	0.30	0.07	-0.08	0.25	0.51	-0.09
Latin America and Caribbean	0.28	2.33	1.44	0.41	-0.62	-1.76	0.32	0.11	-0.27	0.33	0.76	0.00
South Asia	0.25	1.82	0.39	0.34	2.52	1.15	0.37	2.32	1.04	0.31	2.18	0.82
East Asia and Pacific	0.46	3.83	1.18	0.51	3.77	0.71	0.48	4.04	1.58	0.48	3.89	1.21
Middle East and North Africa	0.37	3.75	1.86	0.50	2.50	0.37	0.47	0.92	0.13	0.44	2.37	0.84
Industrialized countries	0.31	3.49	1.75	0.37	1.15	0.01	0.30	1.70	0.80	0.32	2.23	0.96

Source: Extracted from Ndulu and O'Connell, 2003, revised tables 4.2.1, 4.2.3 and 4.2.4.

    * Total factor productivity.

Korea, and investment in infrastructure, were linked to the Cold War. From 1946 to 1978, this aid amounted to $13 billion ($600 per capita), whilst aid to Taiwan Province of China totalled $5.6 billion ($425 per capita) (Arrighi, 2002: 30–31).

No such largesse was showered on the economies of Africa. In all, the Republic of Korea received $6 billion of United States economic aid from 1946 to 1978, compared with $6.89 billion for all of Africa and $14.8 billion for all of Latin America over the same period (Arrighi, 2002: 31).[55] On the other hand, sub-Saharan Africa became the theatre for playing out Cold War confrontations. Misrule and usurpation of state power for private gain could be overlooked, and in some cases even condoned, as in Mobutu's Zaire (Arrighi, 2002: 31; Sindzingre, 2004).

These differences in the "initial conditions" between East Asia and sub-Saharan Africa were accentuated further by the differences in legacies inherited in the domains of state formation and national economic integration. Consequently, these huge disparities in post-colonial economic heritage of political–economic configurations were critical in conditioning the coping strategies or abilities of the two regions in the aftermaths of the oil crises (Arrighi, 2002: 24–26). The Bretton Woods Institutions also need to take some responsibility for sub-Saharan Africa's economic misfortunes in the past quarter century, as evidenced by the disappointing outcome of SAPs. These programmes tended to marginalize domestic capital, with their focus being placed on foreign capital and on privatization (for fiscal reasons) rather than on building domestic productive capacity or empowering the domestic entrepreneurial class.[56] The premature removal of protection in Africa, in terms of duration of import substituting industrialization (ISI) strategies (unlike in Asia) and the absence of policies ("carrots" as well as "sticks") designed to align domestic capital with its developmental role, further undermined the domestic entrepreneurial class.[57] Arguably, the window of opportunity between African independence and the onset of global recession (about 15 to 20 years), was too short for any viable development policy to take shape, or for Africans to learn by doing.

Indeed, it is arguable that the various negative characterizations of the African State have much to do with their economic meltdown starting from about the mid-1970s.[58] The neo-patrimonial State as a theoretical construct has some weaknesses. Certain "clientelistic" practices may be morally reprehensible, but despite recent attempts, there is as yet no robust theoretical framework predicting how they affect the performance of capitalist economies, nor indeed, the extent to which they are pathological to capitalist economic systems.[59] And rent-seeking does not necessarily have to be debilitating to an economic system. If channelled into production, rents can contribute to development in neo-patrimonial States.[60] The issue is that the Asian experience has been idealized to the extent of obscuring the appropriate lessons to be learnt from it. In effect, we have failed to identify correctly the very complex processes that underscore the successful performance of these countries (Mkandawire, 2001). Indeed, this point has been echoed recently by the World Bank in the "Forward" to its recent publication on lessons to be learnt from a decade of reforms: "There was also appreciation and recognition that the complexity and diversity of growth experiences are not amenable to simplistic policy prescriptions. They required more refined and rigorous economic analysis" (World Bank, 2005b: xiii).

The latest attempts by the new institutional economists to attribute the developmental problems of sub-Saharan Africa mainly to a lack of democratic regimes, or a lack of "good governance" (broadly defined) is equally suspect. Some of the earliest developmental States in Asia (the Republic of Korea and Singapore) had authoritarian regimes, although earlier links between authoritarian regimes and development[61] no longer appear credible. On the other hand, democratic regimes do not seem to have a monopoly on fast economic growth and development (e.g. the world's largest democracy, India, has started to experience high levels of growth only recently). Neither do States with strong centralizing tendencies fail to develop, as the case of China illustrates. There is some consensus, however, that in the long run democratic dispensation through opening the political space for a much greater participation of the citizenry and civil society organizations would be most likely to allocate resources in ways that best address the needs of the population.[62]

To sum up, much of the explanation for Africa's economic and political development appears to have been conjectural, rather than robust and rooted in the actual economic and political history of the continent. External factors and institutions have had a much larger sway on Africa's economic and political fortunes than is usually acknowledged. Sometimes, these have had direct adverse consequences for the nature of political and economic governance in some countries, although this is not to absolve entirely the internal debilitating (economic and political) dynamics which were spawned by some of these processes. Overall, a propitious external environment often leads to positive economic outcomes in many African countries. Indeed, African countries proved capable of attaining solid growth rates in such circumstances in the 1960s and early 1970s. And they are poised to seize the opportunity once more, as evidenced by the green shoots of high growth on the back of high commodity prices, underpinned by a strong export demand from Asia, debt relief and, recently, increased aid. Moreover, such recent growth performance can only be improved upon and sustained if African countries promote diversification and increase the technology intensity of their exports.

Considering the improved macroeconomic management as reflected in good macroeconomic fundamentals across the continent (lower levels of inflation and lower fiscal deficits, together with low albeit slowly rising domestic savings), this would appear to be the right moment to nurture the developmental States. The commitment to good governance underpinned by the APRM of NEPAD/African Union, and increasing democratic dispensation, should in all probability support such a State and help ensure that its policies are not hijacked by a minority to serve its selfish interests. Recent analyses confirm that the so-called first order problems – institutions, macroeconomic stability, trade openness, education and inequality – may no longer be binding constraints in Africa (see, for example, Johnson et al., 2007). This highlights the need for policy space, which could be used by countries themselves to identify their priorities and specific challenges, and then design a development strategy that responds to these.

However, there are limits to the comparisons (and perhaps lessons) that can be drawn between the NIEs and Africa. Current conditions in Africa and those initial conditions in the NIEs in the 1950s and 1960s (particularly in the rural economy) may share some similarities, but there are also significant differences. The fact that African economies have suffered from almost a quarter century of stagnation and de-industrialization, and associated informalization of the economy, also suggests caveats for any simple notion of replication of development strategies (UNCTAD, 2006a). At present, most African countries are unable to design their own development strategies because of severe restrictions on their policy autonomy stemming from two main sources. Donors fund a large proportion of the government budget, in some cases more that 50 per cent, so they have a large sway on what policies could be implemented through conditionalities and moral suasion. Secondly, most of these countries are members of WTO, and are therefore constrained by the "single undertaking" commitment entailed by this. An upshot of this is that policy options exercised by the NIEs are no longer available for use by other developing countries, as they are absolutely proscribed. Only a limited number of these policies could be implemented under well-defined and very restricted circumstances.

E. "Policy space" – what to do with it?

Over the past quarter century, the neoliberal economic logic that dictated unbridled liberalization policies has contributed to growing inequality in many parts of the world, including even in some of the new emerging economies (Wade, 2004; Broad and Cavanagh, 2006). The number of people living on less than one dollar per day increased not only in sub-Saharan Africa over this period, but also in Latin America and the Caribbean. In sub-Saharan Africa, the number of people living on less than one dollar per day increased from 167.5 million to 298.3 million between 1981 and 2004; in Latin America and the Caribbean, the number increased from 39.4 million to 47 million over the same period (Chen and Ravallion, 2007).[63] The growth rates of poor countries during the periods of trade liberalization, 1980 to 2000, were much lower than in the period when markets were less open, 1960 to 1980 (Broad and Cavanagh, 2006; Rodrik, 2001a; Easterly, 2001; Arrighi, 2002; Wade, 2004).[64] The view has been echoed by other scholars that "… the real economic performance of countries that had recently adopted Washington Consensus polices … was distinctly disappointing" (Krugman, 1995).

Indeed, as argued by Rodrik, much of the evidence produced on total factor productivity growth supporting the idea of more dynamic inefficiency under an import-substituting regime than under an outward-oriented one is "simply incorrect". This is because "… as an industrialization strategy intended to raise domestic investment and enhance productivity, import substitution apparently worked pretty well in a very broad range of countries until the mid-1970s" (Rodrik, 2001a: 17). As discussed earlier, this was the case in several African countries.

To Rodrik, the ISI approach fell out of favour not only because of the economic collapse of many developing countries following this approach in the 1980s, but also because of the influential studies of some economists (for example, Little et al., 1970; and Balassa, 1971).[65] The ISI economies collapsed due to their failure to adjust their macroeconomic policies to a number of external factors after 1973, including the breakdown in the Bretton Woods fixed exchange rate system, the two major oil shocks, and the commodity boom and bust cycles. Thus, trade and industrial policies were not the real culprits (Rodrik, 2001a), and should therefore not have been the focus of the neoliberals. This is consistent with the observation of others that the cause of the African crisis during this period was "… due primarily to structural and conjunctural processes of the global economy…" rather than to "bad" polices and "poor" governance (Arrighi, 2002: 33). In his analysis of the stagnation in developing countries over almost two decades (1980–1998), Easterly also concludes that worldwide factors (increased world interest rates, debt overhang and growth slowdown in the industrial world, among others) may have contributed to their stagnation. "… [P]oor policies are not a plausible candidate for explaining the lost decades. Polices either got better or remained the same throughout the period, 1960–1998" (Easterly, 2001: 12).

While China and India have recently been the "new recruits" to the neoliberal cause because of their phenomenal growth performance since the 1990s, the experiences of these two countries are anything but lessons in the application of neoliberal economics. Neither of these countries pursued the Washington Consensus blindly. Rather, each reserved some markets to the domestic firms whilst selectively and carefully opening up others. This policy was accompanied in each case by a targeting of resources for land reform, education and other national goals. Thus, the substantial drop in extreme poverty in both countries has been attributed to government policy and not simply to external orientation of the economy (Broad and Cavanagh, 2006).

Contrary to popular perception, advocating the use of government policy to correct some of the egregious excesses of the market is not tantamount to a return to statism or protectionist economic policies. Rather, it is a call to move away from preoccupations with policies based on the ideological divide of "laissez faire" and "dirigisme" to a set of more refined and eclectic policy measures that combine features of both, but tailored to the specific development challenges or circumstances of each country. In other words, it is a move to a kind of "à la carte development policy menu". Some policy measures under this menu would perhaps fall foul of the WTO Agreements, which define current global trade rules. Nevertheless, these agreements are not cast in stone, and several development economists and trade experts have been calling for their review to take into account the peculiar situations prevailing in poor countries (see, for example, UNCTAD, 1998b: 63–84; Das, 2005). There is also some flexibility in these Agreements, although highly restricted in some cases, that poor countries, including those in Africa, could exploit to serve their development objectives. African countries need greater "policy space" to be able to design and implement these policies. Effective rolling back and/or rationalization of conditionalities by the Bretton Woods Institutions would also ensure that space vacated by the WTO Agreements is not encroached upon.

How then should African countries use this "policy space"? No doubt, in attempting to take advantage of the space to be vacated by the multilateral financial institutions, there is the need for caution and avoidance of a return to the "bad old days" that set in immediately after the economic collapse of the late 1970s. For a start, these countries must seek to rely as much as possible on their own resources for investment in the medium term, which suggests greater efforts at domestic resource mobilization[66] and a gradual reduction of dependence on external resources, namely ODA. There is only a perfunctory reference to domestic resource mobilization in NEPAD, without elaborating any specific actions to address it (NEPAD, 2001: 44–45). Both the MDGs and NEPAD give more importance to foreign aid, FDI, ODA, debt relief and trade to attain their objectives. The point is that whilst all these are important, there is a need for a "domestic driver" if a self-sustaining growth and development process is to be realized. Greater domestic mobilization will not only reduce excess reliance on aid and FDI, but will also create a legitimate policy space in which "ownership" is actualized by channelling both aid and investment into fast-growing sectors with huge multiplier or spillover effects for the whole of the economy.

Furthermore, making effective use of this policy space will also necessitate the formulation of a national development (or industrial) strategy that identifies clear objectives, spells out policies to attain them, and has effective monitoring mechanisms to ensure that policy targets are being met. This strategy for rapid self-sustaining growth and development has to be four-pronged. Policies must be designed to promote enhanced domestic resource mobilization; encourage domestic investment; and engender a profit–investment nexus, as well as an export–investment nexus, as a basis for rapid capital accumulation and an export promotion platform. Considering the failure of market forces to promote all these objectives (à la SAPs), attaining them would almost certainly call for more active roles for Governments in the policy area.

F. Concluding remarks

A simple replication of the East Asian developmental State, even if there were such a thing, would not do. As a matter of fact, there is no such thing as the East Asian model of a developmental State that could be recommended to Africa. Indeed, the intrinsic differences among the Asian experiences underscore the importance of "trial and error" as an important ingredient of policy formulation and implementation in developmental States. This process should benefit from constant monitoring and the feeding of the lessons learnt from monitoring into new policies to overcome earlier shortcomings.

The initial conditions are not only different between African countries at present and the NIEs of the 1950s and 1960s, but also different among individual African countries. The global economic context of the 1950s and 1960s, both for the NIEs and for Africa, is also radically different from the current environment. The Cold War has ended, and security concerns are now focused on terrorism; the General Agreement on Tariffs and Trade (GATT) has been replaced with the WTO, whose agreements are binding on all members under its "single undertaking" principle; and there have been major advances in science and technology, including in ICT, which could facilitate "leapfrogging" for the laggards. While the cynic might argue that these developments pose severe challenges for poor developing countries, the optimist might see in these development opportunities worth exploiting.

Thus, whilst we have argued for the nurturing of some form of developmental States in Africa, an acknowledgement of this diversity in initial conditions would call for different policy strands within the context of an overall strategy of a developmental State. Such a strategy should seek to exploit the opportunities in the current global setup, whilst implementing policies that limit the associated costs that inevitably reduce the net benefits. As mentioned, each country should pursue strategies within the context of its own institutional (economic, political and social) arrangements. The challenge for Africa (as for other developing countries), therefore, is not how to copy any model, but how to create "capitalisms" adaptable to the unique opportunities and development challenges in each country (see, for example, Wade, 2003) in an attempt to increase the net benefits.

A challenge of good macroeconomic management is maintaining macroeconomic stability whilst shifting the economy onto a higher growth trajectory, irrespective of the roles played by the private and public sector. Several conditions are indispensable for such an effective macroeconomic management. These include a pro-investment environment predicated on political stability, policy predictability and consistency, and a robust legal and regulatory framework. A competent and technocratic civil service that is independent from politicians, to prevent undue influence in decision-making, is also important, as are coalitions between the domestic entrepreneurial class and the ruling elite. Equally significant is the oversight role of civil society in preventing abuse and misuse of power and/or state resources, and guarding against state capture by narrow business interests. Obviously, it is both more difficult and critical to fulfil these conditions in a developmental State than in other types of States, considering that the "trial and error" nature of policymaking in such States might undermine policy predictability and continuity, and increase the vulnerability of the State to capture by the elite.

The important thing, however, as mentioned earlier, is that a developmental State must be committed to a "development ideology" as a long-term predictable strategy. The escape of sub-Saharan Africa from poverty may be more challenging in the present circumstances than for East Asia, but fatalism is unwarranted (Johnson et al., 2007), and the means of escape could yet be found in the "developmental States" paradigm.

Chapter 4

RECLAIMING AND UTILIZING POLICY SPACE

Africa's economic growth over the last few years has revived the hope that the continent may be emerging from its long period of stagnation. However, the recent rates of growth have not been high enough and sustained for a long enough period in most countries to have made a significant impact on Africa's development. Africa will need to grow by 7 to 8 per cent per annum for up to about 10 years to reach its development targets, particularly that of halving poverty by 2015 as provided for in the MDGs. As mentioned earlier, according to UNCTAD estimates in 2000, investment rates needed to reach 22–25 per cent in order to increase sustainable growth rates to 6 per cent per annum. Investment rates realized by SSA in recent years, 2000 to 2004, averaged only 18.1 per cent of GDP, while the figure for all of Africa was 20.7 per cent. The analysis in this report identifies domestic financial resources as one source that could contribute to closing this resource gap, although these would have to be complemented by ODA and FDI. It also identifies macroeconomic stability, and a stable and predictable policy and political environment, as prerequisites for attracting and sustaining domestic and foreign investments. The role of the State in the support and development of markets and other capitalist institutions is critical. A "strong State" is required for the efficient functioning of these institutions. Indeed, the debate over the direction of development policy in Africa should be underscored by a historical understanding not only of the institutions that underpin the development of markets, but also of the evolution of the State itself in Africa. African countries should choose their development strategies against the background of the available institutional options and their specific historical circumstances (see also Stein, 1994).

The ideas proposed below are some of the elements that could be part of Africa's development strategy with respect to domestic resource mobilization. Some specific measures are proposed with a general but brief discussion of their objectives and modes of implementation. However, the diversity of situations in Africa does not allow for a discussion with finer details. It is expected that UNCTAD's ongoing project on Domestic Resource Mobilization in Africa, which covers seven countries, will provide more details on some of these measures.

A. Mobilizing domestic savings

The discussion in this report shows that there are important resources within African economies which, if properly mobilized and channelled into productive investments, could boost economic performance. Notwithstanding country particularities within Africa, there is a set of common measures that could help countries put in place an institutional setting that is conducive to domestic resource mobilization. In this regard, African countries should implement an arrangement between the Government and the business community, with the objective of identifying the best way to achieve the shared objective of having a financial sector that integrates economic development into its objectives. This would entail the adoption of a financial sector charter that defines the expected contribution of the sector to the national economic development agenda, with clear implementation modalities. Such a charter would provide financial institutions with appropriate incentives to encourage them to maximize their contributions to development, with monitoring guidelines of the performance of the parties involved. The charter could be crafted along the lines of South Africa's "Transformation Charter", agreed between government, business, labour and community representatives in August 2002.[67] The following elements could be part of the new development-oriented financial sector strategy.

Long-term investment fund

Considering the large liquidities in the financial sector of many African economies, countries could consider channelling part of them into a long-term investment fund. It would be funded by voluntary contributions from the most profitable public and private companies, which are often obliged to keep retained profits as short-term bank deposits, due to limited low-risk investments. Pension funds also hold large financial resources that could be partly invested in the long-term investment fund. In resource-rich countries where Governments accumulate rents during periods of high commodity prices, part of the rents could be used to boost the financial base of the fund.

Pooling resources would not only allow for funding large projects, but also minimize the loss incurred by each investor should the investment fail. If necessary, this initiative would benefit from government incentives, in the form of tax breaks, for example, on the amounts contributed to the fund. It could be managed by a board comprising government representatives as well as the major contributors. In the case of Burundi, Nzobonimpa et al. (2006) calculated that if half the profits of the country's eight commercial banks, two development banks, the largest insurance company, a brewery and a sugar factory had been invested in the national economy, they would have increased the country's capital formation from 15 per cent of GDP in 2004 to 23 per cent in 2005. If these resources were spent on productive investment rather than on consumption, their likely effect on inflation would be limited. In the medium term, as development picks up, the development of stock exchanges and bond markets could provide another way of increasing firms' access to long-term investment resources.

Development banks

Development banking has fallen out of favour, owing to past experiences in several countries where they were mismanaged and ended up closing. However, it is important to keep in mind that development banks' past failures were not due to their irrelevance. As discussed in chapter 3, development banks could be an important conduit through which some government development policies are implemented. For example, development banks should refocus their activities on those sectors that are not traditionally attractive to commercial banks. These could include agriculture, non-farm rural activities and small and medium-sized enterprises. The bulk of development banks' financial resources could come from ODA. There are examples in Africa of well-managed development banks that have played a unique role in filling an important financing gap left by commercial banks in some sectors.

Microfinance

African countries could consider creating a microfinance fund dedicated to small credit applicants in urban and rural areas in a way that strengthens the synergies between the formal and informal financial sectors. The fund would use ODA as well as voluntary contributions from the banking sector to constitute its capital. The central bank could also allow commercial banks to contribute a portion of their legal reserves to the fund. In order to encourage commercial banks to contribute to the microfinance fund, interest rates on their contributions could be equal to the rate at which the central bank remunerates their legal reserves plus a risk premium representing some proportion of the difference between the latter and the commercial bank lending rate. This would have the effect of reducing the high interest rates currently paid on micro-credits. Small farmers and small-scale entrepreneurs in need of financial support could be required to open accounts with microfinance institutions with clear repayment mechanisms based on the revenue from the activities of these entrepreneurs. For example, the repayment of these micro-credits could be made contingent on the sale of farmers' crops, with these institutions having a lien on monies from these sales. Requiring the producers to form cooperatives that would be answerable to the microfinance fund could increase enforceability of the repayment mechanism.

Capital repatriation and remittances

Capital flight is the ultimate reflection of a country's failure to mobilize and retain its domestic financial resources. Given the importance of this outflow in a number of African countries, serious consideration should be given to the way these resources could be repatriated and how to limit their flow in the future. Capital flight could be curbed or reversed if African countries generated enough investment opportunities that could interest its diasporas. Countries such as Ethiopia, Rwanda and Ghana have managed to attract diasporas back to invest in their countries of origin. To counter the fear of some potential investors, countries could consider setting a time-bound capital flight amnesty with a "no questions asked" policy on capital repatriation. Moreover, the new United Nations Convention Against Corruption, which has already been ratified by more than 40 African countries, offers an international framework that could be used to plead for the return of the proceeds of corruption.

The key policy issue with respect to remittances is not only how to increase them, but also how to encourage the senders to use formal channels and increase the share allocated to investment rather than to consumption. One novel way adopted by a bank in Burundi is to provide remittance-related financial services at competitive cost. The bank has been organizing campaigns in Europe to invite the diasporas to invest in instruments that will be under the direct management of this commercial bank. In addition, this bank offers to act on behalf of the diasporas who are willing but unable to invest in the country due to their absence. These services are expected to be provided at a relatively low cost if many people join the scheme.

Developed countries from which remittances originate could consider, as a measure of development cooperation, granting tax breaks on the amounts sent home through official channels by diasporas as a way of increasing remittance flows. To reduce transfer costs, developed countries could help by proposing transfer mechanisms that limit transaction costs to the minimum. One way could be to encourage local banks to collect remittances into one account per recipient country, with a proper record of senders' and recipients' addresses. The bank would make one transaction per period to send the total amount into a bank account in a recipient country that would in turn redistribute it to the addresses provided by the sending bank. The advantage of this mechanism is that the remittances would use official channels at very low transfer costs.

B. Developing credit markets and boosting productive investments

Credit is the mechanism through which savings are transformed into investment. However, as chapter 2 has discussed, a vibrant investment sector requires more than just credit; it also needs a conducive investment climate. Therefore, investment strategies must combine the requirements of a viable credit market with a good investment environment. In this regard, policies to boost investment could centre on the following.

Low credit transaction costs

High credit transaction costs, particularly outside urban centres, are one of the key reasons why so many businesses or potential entrepreneurs in Africa do not have access to credit. In cases where the limited geographical bank coverage may be due to cost-benefit considerations, encouraging greater density of financial institutions through incentives such as one-off subsidies could help bring more economic agents into the credit market. Obviously, complementary policies such as infrastructure development in rural areas would be needed to introduce banking services. For example, in many countries, the development of mobile telephony has reduced transaction costs by linking up different market segments geographically separated by infrastructure deficiencies.

A different way of addressing the problem of high transaction costs would be to help, rather than hinder, the work of microfinance institutions. As the report discusses, microfinance institutions should be recognized as holding the key for financial development in rural areas, where they could operate down to one-tenth of formal banks. As a result, formal banks and microfinance institutions should each specialize in their segment but allow for proper communication between the two credit sources. In particular, given that many microcredit institutions' activities are limited by resource constraints, they should be able to borrow from commercial banks on preferential terms to expand their lending activities to small borrowers not covered by formal banks.

Credit information and borrowers' database

The poor endowment of African economies in "information capital" has induced a high cost with economic inefficiencies, and prevented the growth of the financial sector. In particular, the lack of reliable information on the risk profile of borrowers is arguably the most important factor constraining bank lending to poorer households and small businesses. The example of Southern African countries, where private bureaus have financial information covering up to 53 per cent of the adult population, is instructive in this regard. Given that the setting up of a comprehensive borrowers' database might not necessarily be in the interest of any individual financial institution, the costs of setting up and maintaining such a database could be at least partly borne by the State. It would be important that whoever manages such a database guarantees confidentiality of information. Also, this agency should be clearly separated from tax authorities, to address the fear that information could be used for tax purposes.

Legal and regulatory framework

Law and order and a credible legal system that enforces property rights are very important instruments of investor protection. Being inter-temporal, credit and investment require an institutional environment where their outcome can be predicted with some degree of certainty. Economic and political stabilization policies that reduce risk and uncertainty should be at the core of the strategy to attract and retain domestic and foreign investment. Obviously, this shows how difficult the task is, particularly in countries recovering from long periods of internal conflict and instability. In the short term, the creation of credible special commercial courts, sometimes called "fast-track" courts, capable of speeding up procedures in cases relating to investment disputes, could help. In the long term, increasing transparency and simplifying the procedures relating to foreclosure would be necessary to safeguard the interests of investors.

Savings and credit cannot boost investment in a climate that is not friendly to investors, so regulatory measures should also focus on the improvement of the investment climate. Since the investment climate has different dimensions, there are several actions that could be taken to improve it. Firstly, investment requires reliable infrastructure such as roads, electricity and telephone communication.

Putting this infrastructure in place, if necessary on a regional basis, should be a development priority in Africa. Investing in basic infrastructure is the basis for other investments to take place, given the positive effect of infrastructure on investment efficiency. Secondly, unnecessary bureaucratic barriers could be reduced dramatically without any serious adverse effects. For example, if one-window shop policies could be generalized and made more effective, they could reduce drastically the costs due to red tape, as well as opportunities for graft. The simplification of procedures could help reduce entry costs and transaction costs involved in paying taxes, and encourage more informal firms to go into the formal sector, thereby widening the tax base. Moreover, the simplification and rationalization of labour market regulations could help remove a number of old regulations that serve no useful purpose and which may deter the entry of new firms into the formal sector. Thirdly, Governments would gain by re-designing their tax systems to make them simpler by adopting fewer but differential tariff lines for imports of capital or intellectual goods and consumption goods and fairer by relying more on direct taxes. This would also make them more effective and more administratively convenient. Such a new tax policy should be accompanied by efficiency improvements in the use of government revenue as part of a broader policy of improving the relations between the State and society.

C. Delivering appropriate financial and investment policies: the need for a "developmental State"

Most of the challenges to domestic resource mobilization and investment discussed in this report are manifestations of market failures plaguing African economies. This report argues that addressing market failures in Africa requires developmental States that carry out Africa's development agenda. State action could be organized around the following three main objectives: domestic economic integration, strategic external integration, and effective allocation of resources to achieve clear development goals.

Domestic economic integration

The current discourse over the issue of globalization centres on the way economies are or should be integrated into the world economy, with very little consideration given to "internal integration". However, it should be clear from the discussion in this report that African economies first need to be integrated internally before they can integrate gainfully into the world economy. Internal integration means that African economies strengthen their weak domestic linkages, particularly between urban and rural segments, as well as their sectoral input-output linkages. These efforts require sizable investments that can be provided only by the State. Obviously, infrastructure development, particularly that of roads and telephones, is key to internal integration, as it allows different local entities to communicate with each other, and improves the efficiency of the exchange of goods and services – that is, of markets. The State should prioritize investments in the rural economy, given the high multiplier effect and the level of neglect of the rural sector.[68] After all, the rural economy constitutes the basis of national economic activity and accounts for the largest proportion of the population. State intervention, therefore, should foster the integration of rural agricultural and non-agricultural activities. It has been established that the potential for job creation by rural non-agricultural activities is very high in Africa (UNECA, 2005).

Sectoral integration facilitates product diversification and transformation of the national economy. Even some of the highest-growing economies in the continent have not been able to reduce poverty and skewness in income distribution in any remarkable way, because the source of growth has been limited to one or a few isolated activities (e.g. capital-intensive extractive industries operating as enclaves). Thus, new development investments should be carefully judged in terms of their potential contribution to internal integration and productivity growth, within a context of capital accumulation based on a profit-investment nexus. The projects with the highest potential for integration should be given more priority. In addition, diversification of economic activity would limit the adverse effects in terms of trade shocks to international markets. As Wade (2005) argues, diversification rather than specialization, as Africa has been led to believe, appears to be associated with the most successful development experiences in Asia and elsewhere. Policy measures in this regard would have to provide incentives for small and medium-sized firms already engaged in activities in these areas to grow, thereby addressing the issue of the "missing middle" in the African productive sectors. This could be in the form of duty drawbacks, subsidized finance, technological assistance, training, developing managerial skills, and a system linking the management of "economic rents" to performance targets, in order to prevent misuse or abuse.

Strategic external integration

Policies implemented over the past quarter century have prioritized external integration over internal integration, resulting in disarticulation of the internal structures of most economies. It is now time to address this imbalance by designing policies that emphasize a strategic and phased external integration congruent with the overall development strategy of each country. In part, this will require policies that prioritize technological upgrading linked to a strategic promotion of FDI into those sectors synergistically connected to domestic research and development activities and national training programmes or skills formation within an investment-export nexus. As discussed earlier, the flexibilities in the various WTO Agreements should be exploited to maximize the benefits and minimize the costs from pursuing external integration. Where some specific WTO Agreements may frustrate the implementation of policies in accordance with development priorities or strategies, steps should be taken to have this resolved within the framework of the WTO negotiating process. Africa's entry into the global markets will not be easy, given the current level of competitiveness of countries dominating the labour-intensive exports sector. This underscores the challenges ahead and the need to improve productivity levels.

Effective allocation of resources

The responsibility for Africa's failure to achieve high rates of economic growth over the last three decades has often been blamed on its predatory and rent-seeking officials. While part of the responsibility for Africa's economic failure accrues to its political elites, a more insightful analysis suggests that it might not be right to blame them for all the ills of the continent (see chapter 3). The changes in the international world order and the past experience of keeping the State outside the process of development have undoubtedly shown that Africa needs a "strong State" to carry out the continent's development agenda. The failure of the past development model advocated by the Bretton Woods Institutions has illustrated the need for African States to re-engage in the development business from which they had been marginalized. More particularly, the State must define a clear development vision and translate it into actionable policies.

The widespread market failures and high risk, together with the huge financial resources involved in implementing the earlier stages of development, imply that the private sector cannot be expected to play the lead role. The issue is therefore not "intervention versus non-intervention", but which type of intervention is undertaken, and its objective (Stein, 1994: 1,485). The State's strategic intervention is needed to ensure that the country's limited resources are mobilized and allocated in a way that is compatible with its overall development strategy. As was discussed earlier, the State's instruments for intervention include credit allocation policies, official investment and expenditure, and incentives to private sector agents to encourage them to invest in specific sectors.

State intervention does not necessarily imply protectionism, as is often perceived. As practiced in the past by successful developmental States in both developed and developing countries, strategic intervention combines subsidies, protection and free trade in proportions that are determined in accordance with the specific national situation. All industrialized and industrializing economies implemented various forms of protection of their infant industry in early stages of development. However, there should be time limits to protection so that, once an industry becomes reasonably competitive, it should be allowed to face world competition. Overprotection has proved to be counterproductive because it encourages inefficient production systems, as was the case with some import-substitution experiences.

In conclusion, the State needs a number of attributes to play its rightful role in the process of Africa's development. Firstly, in a transparent and competitive political system, the elites should reflect the wishes of their populations in their decisions. The legitimacy of the State is an important prerequisite for its empowerment to act responsibly on behalf of the population. Secondly, the State should be able to define and implement development policies with some degree of flexibility. Because there is no formula to achieve development objectives, state actors should be allowed to experiment with policies. Development should be approached as a learning-by-doing process, so some failures are inevitable. Thirdly, training should be at the centre of development policy. Those in charge of development policy should be well trained to properly deal with the problems they are confronted with. The discourse on Africa's poor economic performance has not given this factor due importance. In the past, many choices made with the best intentions later proved to be ineffective. Empowering the State means that those acting on its behalf have the necessary training and objectivity to design and implement policies that address their country's development challenges.

Notes

1   Starting with the United Nations Financing for Development (FFD) Conference in Monterrey, Mexico in 2002, a series of meetings have been held culminating in the Group of Eight (G8) heads of State meeting in Gleneagles, Scotland, United Kingdom, in 2005, which proposed doubling aid to Africa from its 2004 level to $48 billion a year by 2010. This proposal, together with the one cancelling all multilateral debts of the heavily indebted poor countries, was subsequently endorsed at the United Nations World Summit in New York in 2005 (see UNCTAD, 2006a).

2   In South Africa, one mobile phone banking company, WIZZIT, set up in March 2005 to provide services to those who have difficulty accessing formal financial services, has already acquired over 50,000 customers (Ivatury and Pickens, 2006).

3   In Kenya, for example, the cost of finance was cited as a "major" or "severe" constraint by 80 per cent of small firms. Access to finance similarly affected 56 per cent of small firms (Blattman et al., 2004). In Mozambique, credit problems were rated as the most important constraint affecting firms: 75 per cent of firms there cited access to credit, and 84 per cent cost of credit, as large or severe problems (Nasir et al., 2003).

4   In Kenya, for example, the interest rate paid out on government bonds reached 50 per cent in 1993 (Nkurunziza, 2004).

5   To limit risk, banks are required to respect solvency ratios fixed by the central bank. A bank has excess liquidity when, for a relatively long period, it maintains liquidity well in excess of the amount required by prudential regulations.

6   There is evidence of public investment crowding in private investment. In a cross-country analysis of the determinants of private investment in 41 developing countries covering the period 1980–1999, Levine (2005) found that one per cent of GDP spent by the Government on capital expenditure is associated with a 0.18 per cent increase in private fixed investment the following year. Although this relationship is positive, the effect appears small, particularly given the extent of the need for private investment.

7   For example, the fact that, between 1992 and 2004, 62 per cent of aid to developing countries spent on technical cooperation was directed to social sectors while only 7 per cent was allocated to infrastructure reflects where the donor community puts more emphasis (see UNCTAD, 2006).

8   During the period 2000–2005, Africa's fertility rate was almost twice that of other developing regions. Latin America and the Caribbean and Asia each had 2.5 children per woman, whereas the rate in Africa was five children per woman (UNECA, 2005c).

9   The situation is, however, somewhat complicated as this observation does not take into account the lower life expectancy rates that have been recorded across much of sub-Saharan Africa because of the high incidence of AIDS-related deaths. For example, there have been dramatic declines in life expectancy, particularly in Southern Africa (see Johnson et al., 2007: 33–34).

10   On the characteristics and operations of the different types of microcredit institutions, see Steel et al. (1997). See also http://www.microfinancegateway.org/ for other microfinance models.

11   The multiplier effect is the dynamic by which investment increases incomes of economic agents such as workers and firm owners involved in the production process. Provided the additional incomes are not fully consumed, there is an increase in savings, which

are later reinvested, creating a virtuous cycle of higher investment, higher incomes and higher savings. The accelerator effect refers to the positive effect of economic growth on private fixed investment. An economy in expansion increases global demand, which in turn necessitates an increase in national output. If the economy's total productive capacity cannot cope with this demand, new investments are needed, which induce economic agents to save in order to take advantage of such opportunities. The result is further economic growth due to the multiplier effect.

12 The expression "original sin" was coined by Eichengreen and Hausman (1999) to characterize the financial fragility of developing countries that cannot use their domestic currency to borrow abroad due to their inconvertibility or to borrow long-term domestically due to the lack of domestic long-term credit instruments. This situation creates a currency and a maturity mismatch deriving from the fact that the returns on investments financed by foreign currency are in domestic currency that cannot be used to pay for the debt. The maturity mismatch is the result of the fact that most banks hold short-term deposits that cannot be used to finance long-term investments in the absence of developed bond markets.

13 Irresponsible use of bonds can worsen a Government's debt position. In addition, the use of bonds may crowd out private investment when banks prefer to invest in bonds rather than productive sectors of the economy, as has been observed in some countries.

14 The Gini coefficient is the most widely used measure of income inequality. It ranges from zero to 100. High values mean high inequality. The five most unequal countries in Africa are Namibia with a Gini coefficient of 74, Gabon with 64, South Africa with 62, the Central African Republic with 61 and Lesotho with 58 (see Bigsten and Shimeles, 2003).

15 This communication constraint has, however, recently been reduced by the availability of mobile telephony.

16 This list is dominated by Southern and francophone African countries. It is highly likely that these countries' banking sectors are dominated by South African banks for the first group and French banks for the second.

17 The costs of taxation and regulation are not included, as they apply only to formal sector lending institutions.

18 The Usury Act was originally enacted in 1968 to outline the conditions governing credit transactions in order to fight against usury. Among other things, maximum interest rates were fixed at 25 per cent for loans below Rand 6,000 and 22 per cent for higher amounts. These ceilings were revised in the Usury Act Exemption Notice. The threshold amount of the loan increased from Rand 6,000 to Rand 10,000 and the repayment period was not to exceed 36 months. For details, see http://www.acts. co.za/usury/index.htm.

19 Lending decisions require accurate information about the borrower. This information is about credit history such as the amounts of past loans; and repayment patterns such as late payments, defaults and bankruptcies. This information, sometimes aggregated into a "credit information index", is collected from several sources, including public registries and private bureaus. When banks get this information and find that the applicant is creditworthy, they may decide to lend. However, if such information does not exist or if the lenders do not access it, they do not lend.

20 These barriers are not particular to Africa, but they are more severe in the continent than elsewhere.

21 The cost of entry is the cost of obtaining a permit to operate a firm, which includes fees – the costs of procedures and forms, photocopies, fiscal stamps, legal and notary charges, etc. (Djankov et al., 2002).

22 Unless specified otherwise, the data in this section are from World Bank (2007a). The methodology and assumptions underlying the data are from http://www.doingbusiness. org/MethodologySurveys. One caveat, however: these data should be used with care for two reasons. Firstly, they generally show large differences between Africa and the rest of the developing world, but it is not clear why. Secondly, these data are new, so they are unable to show Africa's progress over time. As discussed earlier, there is no question that economic institutions have improved in Africa in the last few years. Given these limitations, these data should be interpreted as indicative of trends (see Johnson et al., 2007).

23 It seems that some of the procedures are not necessary. They include a license to play music to the public, irrespective of the line of business, performing an official audit at start-up, certification of marital status, etc. For a list of these procedures, see Djankov et al. (2002).

24 These statistics are based on official cost, procedural and time requirements. Bureaucratic delays and corruption are not considered. If they were, it is more likely that they would further increase the cost of entry.

25 The REI is a composite index that attempts to measure the rigidity resulting from regulations on hiring, working hours and firing of workers, which are also composite sub-indices based on several components. REI and its three components take values from zero to 100, with higher values implying more rigid regulations. REI is a simple average of the three sub-indices (see World Bank, 2007c for the detailed methodology).

26 Other countries with a rate of 20 per cent of salary or higher are Algeria, Burkina Faso, Chad, Egypt, Equatorial Guinea, Gabon, Guinea, Guinea-Bissau, Mali, Senegal, Seychelles, Sudan, Togo and Tunisia. Three quarters of the countries in this list are former French colonies, suggesting that they may have inherited France's pro-worker labour regulations.

27 These aspects of investor protection are not very relevant to investors in Africa, where firms are often small and managed by their owners. However, investor protection is highly relevant for foreign investors, including transnational corporations.

28 This practice may be reflective of developing economies but is not limited to them. In the United States, Warner (1977) shows, using evidence relating corporate bankruptcy of railroad firms between 1933 and 1955, that the use of the formal legal system made the case more complex, longer and more expensive than it would have been if creditors had agreed to negotiate directly with their debtors.

29 Note that the taxes considered here are more than income or profit taxes. They also include social security contributions and other labour taxes paid by the employer, property taxes, turnover taxes and other small taxes, such as municipal fees and vehicle and fuel taxes (see World Bank, 2007c).

30 For a detailed analysis of this issue, see UNCTAD (2005).

31 Information on both variables was available for 39 African countries. Three outliers, having recorded extraordinarily high GFCF rates over the period, namely Lesotho,

Mauritania and Sao Tome and Principe, were removed from the data, so figure 5 is based on 36 African countries.

32   The first-tier NIEs are Hong Kong (China), Taiwan Province of China, the Republic of Korea and Singapore; the second-tier NIEs are Malaysia, Thailand and Indonesia.

33   See UNCTAD, 1996a, 1997, and the special issue of *The Journal of Development Studies*, Volume 34, No. 6, August 1998.

34   These elements, except otherwise stated, are extracted from Sindzingre (2004).

35   See the same source for the specific policy components of the reforms.

36   It should be noted, as discussed in the next paragraph, that the reasons for the demise of development banks transcend the enactment of new banking laws.

37   This challenge of translating savings into investment is faced by even those five countries (Algeria, Botswana, the Republic of the Congo, Gabon and Nigeria) that have attained high levels of savings (more than 30 per cent of GDP) in recent years (UNECA, 2007: 6-7). It could however, be argued that excess liquidity in the banking system is mainly caused by central bank monetary policy operations rather than by the banks' inability to convert deposits into loans. In such a case, a solution to the problem would be lower fiscal deficits, which would allow central banks to scale back their open market operations.

38   It should be recalled, however, that NEPAD has been criticized in some quarters as having little enforcement power, unclear responsibilities, and no clear plan of how to translate its broad objectives into well-specified and traceable goals (Funke and Nsouli, 2003). It has also been labelled as a "failure" by one of its founding fathers, the President of Senegal, Abdoulaye Wade (see UNCTAD, 2006a).

39   To date, 26 African countries have signed up to the APRM process. Three countries have completed the process, whilst reviews have been launched in 13 other countries.

40   There is a high risk of default stemming from a lack of collateral, but the main reasons are mostly due to the lack of credit history of most local enterprises. In addition, the weak legal and regulatory system renders foreclosure on assets an arduous and time-consuming, an undertaking most banks are unwilling to initiate (UNCTAD, 1996b; Brownbridge and Gayi, 1999).

41   Fourteen sub-Saharan African countries, for example, have interest rate spreads of more than 10 percentage points, and spreads are as large as 19 and 20 percentage points in Zambia and Malawi (see McKinley, 2005: 24). High spreads are also a function of operating and transactions costs.

42   The causes of imperfections in rural credit markets include shortage of realizable collateral, lack of ancillary institutions (e.g. insurance markets), high co-variant risk among borrowers, and the very severe problems of enforcing repayment of loan contracts (Besley, 1994).

43   See for example, Stulz (1999), and Mishkin (2001). Intriguingly, however, the latter described the use of prudential controls ("restricting how fast the borrowing of banks could grow, [which] might have the impact of substantially limiting capital inflows" as a "form of capital controls" (Mishkin, 2001: 27).

44   See Gemech and Struthers, 2003: 9 for a summary of arguments against financial liberalization.

45   For example, major aspects of the reforms were implemented before macroeconomic stability was attained; and new entry was liberalized before the promulgation of new

Banking Acts that raised minimum capital requirements (see Brownbridge and Gayi, 1999).

46 An early proponent of this hypothesis is Bates (1981). Later apologists include, for example, Frimpong-Ansah (1992), to whom the African state is simply a "vampire"; Chazan (1988) and Rothchild (1994), who propagated extreme views of the African State bordering on the congenitally incurably nature of the disease of the African State; and Chabal and Daloz (1999), who argue provocatively that African political elites thrive on disorder, the norm which has been institutionalized.

47 The rise of neoliberalism is explained by a variety of factors, including the induction of conservative Governments in the United States, the United Kingdom and Germany (then the Federal Republic of Germany), as well as the implosion of the welfare state, the stagflation of Keynesianism and the breakdown of central planning in Eastern Europe. Structurally, Governments have been forced to rethink the link between State–market relationships, and restructure this in favour of "markets" as part of the process of globalization. At the domestic level, state intervention became associated with authoritarianism, thus discrediting state involvement in the economy (Mkandawire, 2001: 294).

48 This fight was between the neoliberal critics of "interventionist" States (led by Anne Kruger) and the structuralists (Chenery and his team) that marked the McNamara era (see Mkandawire, 2001: 303).

49 The only exception is the African Alternative Framework to Structural Adjustment Programmes for Socio-economic Recovery and Transformation put forward by the United Nations Economic Commission for Africa (UNECA). This was not taken seriously by the intellectual and development community at the time, but with hindsight has proved to be a more accurate diagnosis of the African development problem and prescription (see UNECA, 1989).

50 See Mkandawire (2001) for a discussion of this "impossibility" thesis.

51   Even Africa's new political leaders have focused on the economics of nation-building, with their embrace of privatization and attraction of FDI, their initial objection to SAPs notwithstanding (see Mkandawire, 2001).

52 This explanation of Africa's lower TFP has been contended, however. Mkandawire (2001), for example, notes that the higher capital–output ratios in African countries could be due to the poorer infrastructure (relative to those of Asia) and the resource-intensive nature of African exports, and that a widely-cited study on TFP (Young, 1994) suggests that over this period the Republic of Korea had lower TFP than Botswana, Cameroon, Congo, Gabon, Guinea, Lesotho and Zimbabwe, whilst Singapore had a lower TFP than every African country in the sample of 66 countries. A recent econometric work for the period 1960–2000, however, suggests that TFP was higher in sub-Saharan Africa than in East Asia and the Pacific from 1960 to 1964. For all other periods, TFP was much higher in South Asia and East Asia and the Pacific than in sub-Saharan Africa (Ndulu and O'Connell, 2003; see also Table 6 in the text.)

53 Some Asian countries with a strong manufacturing base chose to restrict the increase in their debt indicators by expanding export volume via a variety of export promotion measures and industrial policies. Many other developing countries did not adjust in this way, either because their economies were not sufficiently diversified, or because they deliberately chose not to (UNCTAD, 1998a: 93; see also Balassa, 1981 and 1985; Kuznets, 1988).

54 In sub-Saharan Africa, between 1980 and 1987, debt to GDP ratio rose from 38 per cent to 70 per cent, whilst the debt to export ratio rose from 150 per cent to 325 per cent. Per capita incomes fell by 14 per cent during the period (UNCTAD, 2004).

55 UNCTAD's own calculations show that between 1960 and 2004, Asia received some $40 billion more in aid than Africa; and during the 1960s, almost half of total global aid flows went to Asia, compared with about a quarter to Africa (UNCTAD, 2006b).

56 See, for example, Bangura (1992: 65–66), who asserts that the fact that the market reformers sought to reconstitute the relationship between foreign and local capital, with liberalization strengthening the hands of the former, among other things created opposition to the reforms among a new coalition of middle class professionals, industrial unions, etc.

57 These issues were raised by Mkandawire in his contribution, as a member of a Panel of Experts, to the debate on "The Impact of Foreign Direct Investment in Africa" during the 52nd Session of the Trade and Development Board of UNCTAD at the Palais des Nations on 10 October 2005.

58 See a detailed discussion of some of these issues in Mkandawire (2001: 299–302).

59 On the contrary, some of "clientelist" practices feature in the accumulation strategies of these economies. As an independent variable, neo-patrimonialsm is not robust enough to explain economic low growth if accounts of high corruption in the NIEs, in the wake of the Asian financial crisis, are anything to go by. Neo-patrimonial states, including even those in Africa, have pursued developmental policies. The issue is that the Asian experience has been idealized to the extent of obscuring the appropriate lessons to be learnt from it. In effect, we have failed to identify correctly the very complex processes that underscore the successful performance of these countries (Mkandawire, 2001).

60 Several economists have argued that rents can be both productive and unproductive in their impact on the economy. Where the rent of a firm depends on the volume of its activities, rents become a function of its performance, the pursuit of which can lead to an increase in productivity. Rent-seeking thus becomes a spur to growth as its seekers attempt to capture as much of it as possible (Baumol, 1990; Rodrik, 2001b; Mkandawire, 2001, Sindzingre, 2004). The use of the Asian experience to discredit rent-seeking behaviour as not being consonant with the developmental State is thus not credible (Mkandawire, 2001).

61 The liberal democratic theory establishing a link between economic development and political democracy has been challenged, for example, by O'Donnell (1973), based on the Latin American development experience of the 1960s and 1970s.

62 For example, it has been argued that linking democracy with economic restructuring allows individuals and organizations to pose the question of democratic governance of public resources more sharply, and that this is a more realistic way of launching underdeveloped crisis economies on the paths of stable and sustainable democratization (Bangura, 1992: 82).

63 In terms of the proportion of the population subsisting on one dollar per day or less, the percentage for sub-Saharan Africa remained more or less the same at about 42 per cent over this period, although the figure peaked at about 48 per cent in 1996. The proportion in Latin America and the Caribbean declined slightly, from 10.8 per cent to 8.6 per cent after a peak of 13 per cent in 1984 (Chen and Ravallion, 2007).

64   Easterly (2001), for example, estimates a median per capita growth rate of 2.5 per cent for developing countries over the period 1960–1979, and a 0.0 per cent growth during the period of reforms, 1980–1998.

65   These economists gave much prominence to the trade problems of developing countries allegedly deriving from a conflict between ISI regimes and the growth of exports. They argued that overvalued domestic currencies, the result of tight exchange rate controls and expansionary production policies, favour production for domestic use rather than for exports, and therefore have adverse effects on growth. They brought about a change in the conventional thinking of many economists and policy makers at the time through a series of detailed country studies utilizing cross-country statistical analysis of the ISI process and the interactions between trade and growth; and newly formalized concept of effective rates of protection to compare ISI policies across industries and countries.

66   The Finance for Development Conference (2002) also underscores the need for mobilizing both public and private domestic savings as a basis for fiscal sustainability, within a framework of equitable and efficient tax systems and administration. It notes furthermore that improvements in public spending should not crowd out productive private investment (United Nations, 2002: 2–4).

67   The key objective of the Charter is to promote a competitive financial sector that reflects the country's demographics and contributes to the establishment of an equitable society by providing accessible financial services to the previously excluded segments of the population and by directing investment into targeted sectors of the economy. See http://www.fscharter.co.za/page.php?p_id=1 for details.

68   Rural investments have the potential to increase employment, improve the productivity of land, increase non-agriculture economic activity and induce technological improvements.

References

Addison T, Roe A and Smith M (2006). Fiscal policy for poverty reduction, reconstruction, and growth. WIDER Policy Brief, 5, 2006. Helsinki: World Institute for Development Economics Research.

African Development Bank (AfDB) (2006). *Selected Statistics on African Countries Volume XXV.* Tunis: African Development Bank.

Ajayi S (1997). An analysis of external debt and capital flight in the severely indebted low income countries in sub-Saharan Africa. IMF Working Paper 97/68. Washington DC: International Monetary Fund.

Akyüz Y, Chang H-J, Kozul-Wright R (1998). New perspectives on east Asian development. *The Journal of Development Studies*, 34 (6), August.

Amsden A (1989). *Asia's Next Giant: South Korea and Late Industrialization*, New York, Oxford University Press.

Amsden A (1991). Big business and urban congestion in Taiwan: The origins of small enterprise and regionally decentralized industry. *World Development*, 19 (9).

Amsden A (2001). *The Rise of "The Rest": Challenges to the West from Late-Industrializing Economies*, Oxford University Press, Oxford.

Aron J and Muellbauer J (2000). Personal and corporate saving in South Africa. *World Bank Economic Review*, 14 (3): 509–544.

Arrighi G (2002). The African crisis: world systemic and regional aspects. *New Left Review*, 15: 5–36, May-June.

Aryeetey E (2004). Financing Africa's future growth and development: some innovations. G24 Discussion Paper. http:www.g24.org/aryeetey.pdf/.

Aryeetey E, Baah-Nuakoh A, Duggleby T, Hettige H and Steel W (1994). The supply and demand for finance among SMEs in Ghana. World Bank Discussion Paper 251. Washington DC: World Bank.

Aryeetey E and Udry C (2000). Saving in Sub-Saharan Africa. CID Working Paper No. 38. Cambridge: Harvard University.

Avom D and SML Eyeffa (2006): Quinze ans de restructuration bancaire dans la CEMAC: qu'avons-nous appris? Unpublished manuscript.

Balassa B (1971). *The Structure of Protection in Developing Countries*, John Hopkins University Press, Baltimore.

Balassa B (1981). The Newly Industrializing Developing Countries after the Oil Crisis. Weltwirtschaftliches, Archive, 117 (1): 142–194.

Balassa B (1985). Exports, Policy Choices and Economic Growth in Developing Countries after the First Oil Shock. *Journal of Development Economics*, 18: 23–35.

Bangura Y (1992). Authoritarian rule and democracy in Africa: A theoretical discourse in Gibbon Y, Bangura Y and Ofstad A (eds.) (1992). *Authoritarianism, Democrcay and Adjustment: The Politics of Economic reform in Africa*, Seminar Proceedings No. 26, The Scandinavian Institute of African Studies, Uppsala.

Basu A, Blavy R and Yulek M (2004). Microfinance in Africa: experience and lessons from selected African countries. IMF Working Paper WP/04/174. Washington DC: International Monetary Fund.

Baumol WJ (1990). Entrepreneurship: productive, unproductive and destructive. *Journal of Political Economy*, 98 (5): 893–921.

Bates RH (1981). *States and Markets in Africa*, University of California Press, Berkeley.

Besley T (1994). How Do Market Failures Justify Interventions in Rural Credit Markets? *The World Bank Research Observer*, 9 (1): 27-47.

Besley T and Burgess R (2004). Can labor regulation hinder economic performance? evidence from India. *Quarterly Journal of Economics*, 19 (1): 91–134.

Bigsten A and Shimeles A (2003). Prospects for "pro-poor" growth in Africa. Paper presented at the workshop on Growth Strategies in Eastern Africa, Southern Sub-Regional Office of the United Nations Economic Commission for Africa, December.

Bigsten A and Soderbom M (2005). What have we learned from a decade of manufacturing enterprise surveys in Africa? World Bank Policy Research Working Paper 3798, Washington DC: World Bank.

Bigsten A, Collier P, Dercon S, Gauthier B, Gunning J, Isaksson A, Oduro A, Oostendorp R, Pattillo C, Soderbom M, Sylvain M, Teal F and Zeufack A (1999). Investment in Africa's manufacturing sector: a four country panel data analysis. *Oxford Bulletin of Economics and Statistics*, 61 (4): 489–512.

Bigsten A, Collier P, Dercon S, Fafchamps M, Gauthier B, Gunning J, Oduro A, Oostendorp R, Pattillo C, Soderbom M, Teal F and Zeufack A (2003): Credit Constraints in Manufacturing Enterprises in Africa. *Journal of African Economies*, 12 (1): 104–125.

Blattman C, Cotton L, Desai V, Eldabawi I, Habyarimana J, Marchat J-M, Ramachandran V, Kedia Shah M, Ajayi J, Kimuyu P, Ngugi R, Bigsten A and Söderbom M (2004). Enhancing the competitiveness of Kenya's manufacturing sector: the role of the investment climate. *World Bank RPED Investment Climate Assessment*, Washington DC: World Bank.

Boyce JK and Ndikumana L (2001). Is Africa a net creditor? new estimates of capital flight from highly indebted sub-Saharan African countries, 1970–1996. *Journal of Development Studies*, 38 (2): 27–56.

Brimmer AF (1971). Central banking and economic development: the record of innovation. *Journal of Money, Credit and Banking*, 3 (4): 780–792, November.

Broad R and Cavanagh J (2006). The hijacking of the development debate: How Friedmand and Sachs got it wrong. *World Policy Journal*, Summer.

Brownbridge M and Gayi S (1999). Progress, constraints and limitations of financial sector reforms in the least developed countries. Finance and Development Research Programme Paper No.7. Manchester: Institute for Development Policy and Management.

Capasso S (2006). Stock market development and economic growth. WIDER Research Paper 2006/102. Helsinki: World Institute for Development Economics Research.

Castells M (1992). Four Asian Tigers with a dragon head: a comparative analysis of the state, economy and society in the Asian Pacific Rim, in Henderson R and Applebaum J (eds.), *State and Development in the Asian Pacific Rim*: 33–70, London: Sage.

Chabal P and Daloz J-P (1999). *Africa Works: Disorder as Political Instrument*, London: James Currey.

Chang H-J (2002). *Kicking Away the Ladder - Development Strategy in Historical Perspective*. London: Anthem Press.

Chazan N (1988). Patterns of state-society incorporation and disengagement, in Chazan N and Rothchild D (eds.), *The Precarious Balance: State and Society in Africa*, Boulder Co.: Westview Press.

Chen S and Ravallion M (2007). Absolute poverty measures for the developing world, 1981–2004. World Bank Working Paper 4211, Development Research Group, Washington DC: World Bank.

Collier P, Hoeffler A and Pattillo C (2001). Flight capital as a portfolio choice. *World Bank Economic Review*, 15 (1): 55–80.

Collier P, Hoeffler A and Pattillo C (2004). Africa's exodus: capital flight and the brain drain as portfolio decisions. *Journal of African Economies*, 13 (Suppl. 1: ii15–ii54, AERC.

Collier P and O'Connell SA (2007). Opportunities and Choices, in *The Political Economy of Economic Growth in Africa*, 1960–2000. Edited by Ndulu B, O'Connell SA, Bates RH, Collier P and Soludo C, 1, Chap. 2, Cambridge University Press, forthcoming.

Collins SM and Bosworth B (2003). *The Empirics of Growth: An Update*. Washington DC, Brookings Institution, manuscript.

Commission for Africa (CFA) (2005). *Our Common Interest: Report for the Commission for Africa*. London: Department for International Development, Commission for Africa.

Culpeper R (2006). Creating fiscal space through improved domestic resource mobilization in low-income countries. Policy Space in Developing Countries, DONDAD/UN-DESA Roundtable, New York, 7-8 December.

Das BL (2005). *The Current Negotiations in the WTO: Options, Opportunities and Risks for Developing Countries*, London and New York: Zed Books.

Daumont R, LeGall F and Leroux F (2004). Banking in sub-Saharan Africa: what went wrong?, IMF Working Paper WP/04/55, Washington DC: International Monetary Fund.

Deaton A (1990). Saving in Developing Countries: Theory and Review. *Proceedings of the World Bank Annual Conference on Development Economics 1989*, Washington DC: World Bank.

Dercon S (2002). Income Risk, Coping Strategies and Safety Nets. WIDER Research Paper 2002/22, Helsinki: World Institute for Development Economics Research.

DiJohn J (2006). The political economy of taxation and tax reform in developing countries. WIDER Research Paper 2006/74. Helsinki: World Institute for Development Economics Research.

Djankov S, La Porta R, Lopez de Silanes F and Shleifer A. (2002). The regulation of entry. *Quarterly Journal of Economics*, February.

Easterly W (2001). The lost decades: developing countries' stagnation in spite of policy reform 1980–1998, *Journal of Economic Growth*, 6 (2): 135–157.

Eichengreen B and Hausman R (1999). Exchange rate and financial fragility. NBER Working Paper 10036.

Eldabawi I and Mwega F (2000). Can Africa's saving collapse be reversed? *The World Bank Economic Review*, 14 (3): 415–443.

Epstein G (2005). Central banks as agents of development. PERI Working paper series No. 104, Political Economy Research Institute, University of Massachusetts.

Evans P (1995). *Embedded Autonomy: States and Industrial Transformation*. Princeton, NJ: Princeton University Press.

Fafchamps M (1996). The enforcement of commercial contracts in Ghana. *World Development*, 24: 427–448.

Fafchamps M, Gunning J, and Oostendorp R (2000). Inventories and risk in African manufacturing. *The Economic Journal*, 110 (466): 861–893.

Fei J and Ranis G (1975). A model of growth and employment in the open dualistic economy: the cases of Korea and Taiwan, in F. Stewart (ed.) *Employment, Income Distribution and Development*, London: Frank Cass.

Fjeldstad O-H (2005). Corruption in tax administration: lessons from institutional reforms in Uganda. CMI Working Papers, Bergen, Norway.

Fjeldstad O-H (2006). To pay or not to pay? Citizen's views on taxation by local authorities in Tanzania. Research on Poverty Alleviation Special Paper 06.18. Dar Es Salaam: Research on Poverty Alleviation (REPOA).

Fjeldstad O-H and Semboja J (2001). Why people pay taxes: the case of the development levy in Tanzania. *World Development*, 29 (12): 2059–2074.

Fjeldstad O-H and Rakner L (2003). Taxation and tax reform in developing countries: illustrations from Africa. *Chr. Michelsen Institute Report* R2003:6. Bergen: Chr. Michelsen Institute.

Frimpong-Ansah JH (1992). The Vampire State in Africa: *The Political Economy of Decline*, Trenton, NJ: Africa World Press.

Funke N and Nsouli SM (2003). The New Partnership for Africa's Development (NEPAD): opportunities and challenges. IMF Working Paper WP/03/69. Washington DC: International Monetary Fund.

Garson J (2006). *Rethinking the Role of Banks and of Sub-regional and National Development Finance Institutions in Africa*, Financing for Development Office (UN DESA) Regional Consultation, organized by the Agence Française de Développement, 27–28 June, Paris, France.

Gauthier B and Gersovitz M (1997). Revenue erosion through exemption and evasion in Cameroon, 1993. *Journal of Public Economics*, 64: 407–424.

Gauthier B and Reinikka R (2006). Shifting tax burdens through exemption and evasion: an empirical investigation of Uganda. *Journal of African Economies*, 15 (3): 373–398.

Gemech F and Struthers J (2003). The McKinnon-Shaw hypothesis: thirty years on: a review of recent developments in financial liberalization theory. Paper presented at the Development Studies Association (DSA) Annual Conference on Globalisation and Development, Glasgow, Scotland, September.

Griffith-Jones S (with Cailloux J and Pfaffezeller S) (1998). The East Asian financial crisis: a reflection on its cause, consequences and policy implications. Institute of Development Studies, Discussion paper 367.

Gupta S, Pattillo C and Wagh S (2007). Impact of remittances on poverty and financial development in sub-Saharan Africa. IMF Working Paper WP/07/38. Washington DC: International Monetary Fund.

Honohan P and Beck T (2007). *Making Finance Work for Africa*. Washington DC: World Bank.

Hussein K and Thirlwall A (1999). Explaining differences in the domestic savings ratio across countries: a panel data study. *The Journal of Development Studies*, 36 (1): 31–52.

Ikhide S (1996). Commercial bank offices and the mobilisation of private savings in selected sub-Saharan African countries. *The Journal of Development Studies*, 33 (1): 117–132.

International Labour Organization (ILO) (2007). *African Employment Trends*. Geneva: International Labour Organization, April.

IMF (2007). *International Financial Statistics and Balance of Payments Statistics*, CD-ROM, March.

Ivatury G and Pickens M (2006). Mobile phone banking and low-income customers: evidence from South Africa. Paper prepared for the Consultative Group to Assist the Poor. Washington DC: CGAP.

Johnson S, Ostry J and Subramanian A (2007). The prospect for sustained growth in Africa: benchmarking the constraints. NBER Working Paper 13120. Cambridge MA: National Bureau of Economic Research.

Jomo KS (2005). Malaysia's September 1998 controls: background, context, impacts, comparisons, implications, lessons. G-24 Discussion Paper series, No. 36, March.

Khor M. (2005). *The Malaysian experience in financial-economic crisis management: An alternative to the IMF-style approach*, TWN Global Economy series, No. 6.

Krugman P (1995). Dutch tulips and emerging markets. *Foreign Affairs*, 74 (4): 23–44.

Kuznets PW (1988). An East Asian model of economic development: Japan, Taiwan and South Korea. *Economic Development and Cultural Change*, 36 (3): S11–S43.

Lafourcade A-L, Isern J, Mwangi P and Brown M (2005). *Overview of the outreach and financial performance of microfinance institutions in Africa.* Washington DC: Microfinance Information Exchange. http://www.mixmarket.org/medialibrary/mixmarket/Africa_Data_Study.pdf.

Lensink R, Hermes N and Murinde V (2000). Capital flight and political risk. *Journal of International Money and Finance*, 19 (1): 73–92.

Levine E (2005). The crowding-in effect of public investment on private investment. Draft Background Paper on the Macroeconomics of Poverty Reduction, UNDP.

Little I, Scitovsky T and Scott M (1970). *Industry and Trade in some Developing Countries*, London and New York: Oxford University Press for OECD.

Loayza N, Schmidt-Hebbel K and Servén L (2000). Saving in developing countries: an overview. *The World Bank Economic Review*, 14 (3): 393–414.

Mbabazi P and Taylor I (2005). Botswana and Uganda as developmental States. in Mbabazi P and Taylor I (eds.) *The Potentiality of 'Developmental States' in Africa: Botswana and Uganda Compared*: 1–15. Dakar: CODERISA.

McKinley T (2005). Economic Alternatives for Sub-Saharan Africa: "Poverty Traps", MDG-based Strategies and Accelerated Capital Accumulation. Draft Paper for the G-24 Meeting, 15–16 September.

McKinnon RI (1973). *Money and Capital in Economic Development*, Washington DC: The Brookings Institute.

McLiesh C and Ramalho R (2006). *Paying Taxes: The Global Picture*. Doing Business Project, Pricewaterhouse Coopers and the World Bank, downloaded from the World Wide Web.

Meagher P and Wilkinson B (2002). Filling the gap in South Africa's Small and Micro Credit Market: An Analysis of Major Policy, Legal and Regulatory Issues. Paper No. 02/11 (August), Centre for Institutional Reform and the Informal Sector (IRIS) at the University of Maryland.

Mishkin FS (2001). Financial policies and the prevention of financial crises in emerging market countries. NBER Working Paper, No. 8087, January.

Mkandawire T (2001). Thinking about developmental state in Africa. *Cambridge Journal of Economics*, 25 (3): 289–313, May.

Myint H (1982). Comparative analysis of Taiwan's economic development with other countries, in *Experiences and Lessons of Economic Development in Taiwan*, Taipei: Institute of Economics, Academia Sinica.

Myrdal G (1968). *Asian Drama: An Inquiry into the Recovery of Nations*, New York: Pantheon.

Nasir J, de Barros G, Wagle D, Kedia Shah M, Leechor C, Srivastava P, Harding A and Ramachandran V (2003). Mozambique industrial performance and investment climate 2003. *World Bank RPED Investment Climate Assessment*, Washington DC: World Bank.

Ndulu B and O'Connell S (2003). Revised Collins/Bosworth growth accounting decompositions. AERC Explaining African Economic Growth Project Paper. African Economic Research Consortium, March.

NEPAD (2001). *The New Partnership for Africa's Development (NEPAD)*, NEPAD Secretariat, October.

Nissanke M (2001). Financing enterprise development in sub-Saharan Africa. *Cambridge Journal of Economics*, 25 (3): 343–367.

Nissanke M and Aryeetey E (1998). Financial Integration and Development in Sub-Saharan Africa, Liberalisation and Reform in sub-Saharan Africa, London and New York: Routledge.

Nissanke M and Aryeetey E (2006). Institutional analysis of financial market fragmentation in sub-Saharan Africa. WIDER Research Paper No. 2006/87. Helsinki: World Institute for Development Economics Research.

Nkurunziza J (2004). *The Effect of Credit on Firm Growth and Survival in Kenyan Manufacturing*, thesis submitted for the degree of Doctor of Philosophy in the Department of Economics, University of Oxford, Trinity.

Nkurunziza J (2005a). Credit can precipitate firm failure: evidence from Kenyan manufacturing in the 1990s. Centre for the Study of African Economies Working Paper, WPS/2005-05, Oxford University.

Nkurunziza J (2005b). Reputation and credit without collateral in Africa's formal banking. Centre for the Study of African Economies Working Paper, WPS/2005-02, Oxford University.

Nzobonimpa O, Nkurunziza J and Ndikumana L (2006). Promoting a development-oriented financial system in Burundi. Paper prepared for the African Economic Research Consortium, June.

Nyamnjoh F and Malizani-Jimu I (2005). Success or failure of developmental States in Africa: Exploring Africa's experimentation at developmentalism, in Mbabazi P and Taylor I (eds.) *The Potentiality of 'Developmental States' in Africa: Botswana and Uganda Compared*: 16-32. Dakar: CODERISA.

O'Donnell GA (1973). *Modernisation and Bureaucratic Authoritarianism: Studies in South American Politics*, Institute of International Studies, Berkeley: University of California Press.

OECD (2007). OLISNET online Statistical Database, May.

OXFAM (2007). The world is still waiting: broken G8 promises are costing millions of lives. *OXFAM Briefing Paper* 103, Oxford: OXFAM.

Piancastelli M (2001). Measuring the tax effort of developed and developing countries. cross country panel data analysis – 1985/95. *Texto Para Discussão* No. 818. Rio de Janeiro: Ministério Do Planejamento, Orçamento e Gestão.

Pieper U (2000). Deindustrialization and the social and economic sustainability nexus in developing countries: Cross-country evidence in productivity and employment. *Journal of Development Studies* 36 (4): 66–99.

Rodrik D (1997). Where did all the growth go? External shocks, social conflict and growth collapses. http://ksghome.harvard.edu/~drodrik/conftext.pdf (assessed 12 April 2007).

Rodrik D (2001a). *The Global Governance of Trade as if Development Really Mattered.* Background paper commissioned by UNDP as part of the Trade and Sustainable Human Development Project, October.

Rodrik D. (2001b). Institutions, integration and geography: in search of the deep determinants of economic growth, introduction. Conference on the Analytical Country Studies on Growth, Cambridge, MA: Harvard University, Centre for International Development, August.

Rodrik D (2006). Goodbye Washington Consensus, Hello Washington Confusion? A review of the World Bank's "Economic Growth in the 1990s: Learning from a Decade of Reform". *Journal of Economic Literature*, 44 (4): 973–987.

Rothchild D (1994). Structuring state–society relations in Africa, in Widner, J (ed.), *Economic Change and Political Liberalization in Sub-Saharan Africa*, Baltimore: Johns Hopkins University Press.

Salisu M (2005). The role of capital flight and remittances in current account sustainability in sub-Saharan Africa. Paper presented at the Workshop on Capital Flows and Current Account Sustainability in African Economies, organized by the United Nations Economic Commission for Africa in Accra, Ghana, 21–22 September.

Sander C and Maimbo S (2003). Migrant labor remittances in Africa: Reducing obstacles to development contributions. Africa Region Working Paper No. 64. Washington DC: World Bank.

Senbet L and Otchere I (2005). Financial sector reforms in Africa: perspectives on issues and policies. Paper prepared for the Annual World Bank Conference on Development Economics, Dakar, Senegal, January.

Schmidt-Hebbel K, Serven L and Solimano A (1994). Saving, investment, and growth in developing countries, an overview. World Bank Policy Research Working Paper 1382. Washington DC: World Bank.

Shaw E (1973). *Financial Deepening in Economic Development*, New York: Oxford University Press.

Sindzingre AN (2004). Bringing the developmental state back in: contrasting development trajectories in sub-Saharan Africa and East Asia. Paper presented at the 16th Annual meeting of the Society for the Advancement of Socio-Economics (SASE), Washington DC: George Washington University.

Solimano A (2003). Remittances by emigrants: issues and evidence. WIDER Research Paper No. 2003/89. Helsinki: World Institute for Development Economics Research.

Stallings B (2004). The Need for a More Flexible Approach to Development, in (eds.) *Diversity in Development – Reconsidering the Washington Consensus*, The Hague: FONDAD, December, www.fondad.org.

Steel W, Aryeetey E, Hettige H and Nissanke M (1997). Informal financial markets under financial liberalization in four African countries. World Development, 25 (5): 817–830.

Stein H (1994). Theories of Institutions and Economic Reform in Africa. *World Development*, (22) 12: 1833–1849.

Stiglitz (2000). Liberalization, Moral Hazard in Banking and Prudential Regulation: Are Capital Requirements Enough? *American Economic Review*, 90 (1): 147-165, March.

Stotsky J and WoldeMariam A (1997). Tax effort in sub-Saharan Africa. IMF Working Paper WP/97/107. Washington DC: International Monetary Fund.

Stulz R (1999). Globalization of capital markets and the cost of capital. *Journal of Applied Corporate Finance*, 12 (3): 8–25.

Suehiro A (2001). Family business gone wrong? Ownership patterns and corporate performance in Thailand. Asian Development Bank Working Paper 19. Tokyo.

Tanzi V and Zee H (2000). Tax policy for emerging markets: developing countries. IMF Working Paper WP/00/35. Washington DC: International Monetary Fund.

Taylor L (2007). Review "Making Globalization Work", by Joseph E. Stiglitz. *Challenge*, 50 (1): 115–123.

The Economist (2007). The non-aligned movement. 4 April.

Thirlwall A (2003). Growth and Development: With Special Reference to Developing Economies. 7th Edition. Basingstoke: Palgrave MacMillan.

Thirlwall A (2004). The structure of production, the balance of payments and growth in developing countries. Paper presented at UNCTAD workshop, Geneva, 22 November.

United Nations (2002). *Report of the International Conference on Financing for Development*, Monterrey, Mexico. 18–22 March, New York, UN Report, A/CONF. 198/11.

UNCTAD (1996a). *Trade and Development Report, 1996*. United Nations publication, sales no. E.96.II.D.6, New York and Geneva.

UNCTAD (1996b). *World Investment Report 1996 – Investment, Trade, and International Policy Arrangements*. United Nations publication, sales no. E.96.II.A.14, New York and Geneva.

UNCTAD (1997). *Trade and Development Report, 1997*. United Nations publication, sales no. E.97.II.D.8, New York and Geneva.

UNCTAD (1998a). *Trade and Development Report, 1998*. United Nations publication, sales no. E.98.II.D.6, New York and Geneva.

UNCTAD (1998b). *The Least Developed Countries 1998 Report*, United Nations publication, sales no. E.98.II.D.11, New York and Geneva.

UNCTAD (1999). *UNCTAD's Contribution to the Implementation of the United Nations New Agenda for the Development of Africa in the 1990s: African Transport Infrastructure, Trade and Competitiveness*. Report by the UNCTAD secretariat to the Trade and Development Board, Geneva, October.

UNCTAD (2000a). *Capital Flows and Growth in Africa*. UNCTAD/GDS/MDPB/7. New York and Geneva: United Nations.

UNCTAD (2000b). *Trade and Development Report, 2000*. United Nations publication, sales no. E.00.II.D.19, New York and Geneva.

UNCTAD (2001). *Economic Development in Africa: Performance, Prospects and Policy Issues*. New York and Geneva: United Nations.

UNCTAD (2002). *Economic Development in Africa: From Adjustment to Poverty Reduction: What is New?* United Nations publication, sales no. E.02.II.D.18. New York and Geneva.

UNCTAD (2003). *Economic Development in Africa: Trade Performance and Commodity Dependence*. United Nations publication, sales no. E.03.II.D.34. New York and Geneva.

UNCTAD (2005). *Economic Development in Africa: Rethinking the Role of Foreign Direct Investment*. United Nations publication, sales no. E.05.II.D.12. New York and Geneva.

UNCTAD (2006a). *Economic Development in Africa: Doubling Aid: Making the "Big Push" Work*. United Nations publication, sales no. E.06.II.D.10. New York and Geneva.

UNCTAD (2006b) *World Investment Report 2006 – FDI from Developing and Transition Economies: Implications for Development*. United Nations publication, sales no. E.06. II.D.11. New York and Geneva.

United Nations Development Programme (UNDP) (2005). *The potential role of remittances in achieving the Millennium Development Goals – an exploration*. Roundtable on Remittances and the MDGs Background Note, 10 October.

United Nations Economic Commission for Africa (UNECA) (1989). *African Alternative Framework to Structural Adjustment Programmes for Socio-economic Recovery and Transformation*, Addis Ababa: UNECA.

UNECA (2005a). *The Millennium Goals in Africa: Progress and Challenges*. Addis Ababa: UNECA.

UNECA (2005b). *Ministerial Statement of the Thirty-eighth session of the Commission/ Conference of African Ministers of Finance, Planning and Economic Development, Abuja, 14-15 May*. http://www.uneca.org/conferenceofministers/2005/ministerial_statement. htm.

UNECA (2005c): *Economic Report on Africa 2005: Meeting the Challenges of Unemployment and Poverty in Africa*. Addis Ababa: UNECA.

UNECA (2006). *Economic Report on Africa 2006: Capital Flows and Development Financing in Africa*. Addis Ababa: UNECA.

UNECA (2007). *Economic Report on Africa 2007: Accelerating Africa's Development through Diversification*. Addis Ababa: UNECA.

UNESCO (2004). UIS Bulletin on Science and Technology Statistics, Issue No. 1, April.

Wade RH (1990). *Governing the Market: Economic Theory and the Role of Government in East Asian Industrialisation*, Princeton, NJ: Princeton University Press.

Wade RH (2003). *Governing the Market: Economic Theory and the Role of Government in East Asian Industrialization*, Princeton, NJ: Princeton University Press.

Wade RH (2004). Is globalization reducing poverty and inequality? *World Development*, 32 (4): 567–589.

Wade RH (2005). Failing states and cumulative causation in the world system. *International Political Science Review*, 26 (1): 17–36.

Warner JB (1977). Bankruptcy costs: some evidence. *Journal of Finance*, 32 (2): 337–347.

World Bank (1981). *Accelerated Development in Sub-Saharan Africa: An Agenda for Action*, Washington DC: The World Bank.

World Bank (1993). *The East Asian Miracle: Economic Growth, and Public Policy*. Washington DC: The World Bank, September.

World Bank (2004). *World Development Report, 2004: Making Services Work for Poor People*, Washington DC: The World Bank, September.

World Bank (2005a). *African Development Indicators 2005*, CD-ROM.

World Bank (2005b). *Economic Growth in the 1990s – Learning from a Decade of Reform*. Washington DC: World Bank.

World Bank (2006). *African Development Indicators 2006*. Washington DC: The World Bank.

World Bank (2007a). *World Development Indicators*. Washington DC: The World Bank.

World Bank (2007b). Lesotho: an assessment of the investment climate. *World Bank RPED Investment Climate Assessment*, Washington DC: The World Bank.

World Bank (2007c). *Doing Business 2007* (dataset on business environment).

World Economic Forum (2006). *Building on the Monterrey Consensus: The Untapped Potential of Development Finance Institutions to Catalyse Private Investment*, World Economic Forum, Financing for Development Initiative.

Wright G (1999). A critical review of savings services in Africa and elsewhere. Mimeo prepared for Microsave, Nairobi.

Xaba J, Horn P and Motala S (2002). The informal sector in sub-Saharan Africa. Working Paper on the Informal Economy, Employment Sector 2002/10. Geneva: ILO.

Young A (1994). Lessons from East Asia NICs: A contrarian view, *European Economic Review*, 38 (3-4): 964–973.

Economic Development in Africa series:

2000   *Capital Flows and Growth in Africa* –TD/B/47/4–UNCTAD/GDS/MDPB/7
Contributors: Yilmaz Akyüz, Kamran Kousari (team leader), Korkut
Boratav (consultant).

2001   *Performance, Prospects and Policy Issues*–UNCTAD/GDS/AFRICA/1
Contributors: Yilmaz Akyüz, Kamran Kousari (team leader), Korkut
Boratav (consultant).

2002   *From Adjustment to Poverty Reduction:What is New?*–UNCTAD/GDS/
AFRICA/2
Contributors: Yilmaz Akyüz, Kamran Kousari (team leader), Korkut
Boratav (consultant).

2003   *Trade Performance and Commodity Dependence* – UNCTAD/GDS/
AFRICA/2003/1
Contributors: Yilmaz Akyüz, Kamran Kousari (team leader), Samuel
Gayi.

2004   *Debt Sustainability: Oasis or Mirage?* – UNCTAD/GDS/AFRICA/2004/1
Contributors: Kamran Kousari (team leader), Samuel Gayi, Bernhard
Gunter (consultant), Phillip Cobbina (research).

2005   *Rethinking the Role of Foreign Direct Investment* – UNCTAD/GDS/
AFRICA/2005/1
Contributors: Kamran Kousari (team leader), Samuel Gayi, Richard
Kozul-Wright, Phillip Cobbina (research).

2006   *Doubling Aid: Making the "Big Push" Work* – UNCTAD/GDS/
AFRICA/2006/1
Contributors: Kamran Kousari (team leader), Samuel Gayi, Richard
Kozul-Wright, Jane Harrigan (consultant), Victoria Chisala (research).

Copies of the series of reports on *Economic Development in Africa* may be
obtained from the Office of the Special Coordinator for Africa, Division
for Africa, Least Developed Countries and Special Programmes, UNCTAD,
Palais des Nations, CH-1211 Geneva 10, Switzerland (fax: 022 917 0274;
e-mail: africadev@unctad.org). The reports are also accessible on the
website http://www.unctad.org.